MznLnx

Missing Links Exam Preps

Exam Prep for

Managing: A Competency-Based Approach

Hellriegel, Jackson, & Jr., 11th Edition

The MznLnx Exam Prep is your link from the texbook and lecture to your exams.
The MznLnx Exam Preps are unauthorized and comprehensive reviews of your textbooks.

All material provided by MznLnx and Rico Publications (c) 2010
Textbook publishers and textbook authors do not particpate in or contribute to these reviews.

MznLnx

Rico Publications

Exam Prep for Managing: A Competency-Based Approach
11th Edition
Hellriegel, Jackson, & Jr.

Publisher: Raymond Houge
Assistant Editor: Michael Rouger
Text and Cover Designer: Lisa Buckner
Marketing Manager: Sara Swagger
Project Manager, Editorial Production: Jerry Emerson
Art Director: Vernon Lowerui

Product Manager: Dave Mason
Editorial Assitant: Rachel Guzmanji
Pedagogy: Debra Long
Cover Image: Jim Reed/Getty Images
Text and Cover Printer: City Printing, Inc.
Compositor: Media Mix, Inc.

(c) 2010 Rico Publications

ALL RIGHTS RESERVED. No part of this work covered by the copyright may be reproduced or used in any form or by an means--graphic, electronic, or mechanical, including photocopying, recording, taping, Web distribution, information storage, and retrieval systems, or in any other manner--without the written permission of the publisher.

Printed in the United States
ISBN:

For more information about our products, contact us at:
Dave.Mason@RicoPublications.com

For permission to use material from this text or product, submit a request online to:
Dave.Mason@RicoPublications.com

Contents

CHAPTER 1
Developing Managerial Competencies — 1

CHAPTER 2
Learning from the History of Management Thought — 7

CHAPTER 3
Ethics and Social Responsibility — 17

CHAPTER 4
Assessing the Environment — 24

CHAPTER 5
Managing Globally — 33

CHAPTER 6
Fostering Entrepreneurship — 43

CHAPTER 7
Formulating Plans and Strategies — 47

CHAPTER 8
Fundamentals of Decision Making — 56

CHAPTER 9
Using Planning and Decision Aids — 61

CHAPTER 10
Achieving Organizational Control — 69

CHAPTER 11
Designing Organizations — 83

CHAPTER 12
Guiding Organizational Change and Innovation — 87

CHAPTER 13
Managing Human Resources — 96

CHAPTER 14
Motivating Employees — 108

CHAPTER 15
Dynamics of Leadership — 115

CHAPTER 16
Communicating Effectively — 120

CHAPTER 17
Working in Teams — 122

CHAPTER 18
Understanding Organizational Culture and Cultural Diversity — 126

ANSWER KEY — 132

TO THE STUDENT

COMPREHENSIVE

The *MznLnx* Exam Prep series is designed to help you pass your exams. Editors at MznLnx review your textbooks and then prepare these practice exams to help you master the textbook material. Unlike study guides, workbooks, and practice tests provided by the texbook publisher and textbook authors, *MznLnx* gives you **all** of the material in each chapter in exam form, not just samples, so you can be sure to nail your exam.

MECHANICAL

The MznLnx Exam Prep series creates exams that will help you learn the subject matter as well as test you on your understanding. Each question is designed to help you master the concept. Just working through the exams, you gain an understanding of the subject--its a simple mechanical process that produces success.

INTEGRATED STUDY GUIDE AND REVIEW

MznLnx is not just a set of exams designed to test you, its also a comprehensive review of the subject content. Each exam question is also a review of the concept, making sure that you will get the answer correct without having to go to other sources of material. You learn as you go! Its the easiest way to pass an exam.

HUMOR

Studying can be tedious and dry. MznLnx's instructional design includes moderate humor within the exam questions on occassion, to break the tedium and revitalize the brain

Chapter 1. Developing Managerial Competencies

1. _____ is a method by which the job performance of an employee is evaluated _____ is a part of career development.

_____s are regular reviews of employee performance within organizations

Generally, the aims of a _____ are to:

- Give feedback on performance to employees.
- Identify employee training needs.
- Document criteria used to allocate organizational rewards.
- Form a basis for personnel decisions: salary increases, promotions, disciplinary actions, etc.
- Provide the opportunity for organizational diagnosis and development.
- Facilitate communication between employee and administraton
- Validate selection techniques and human resource policies to meet federal Equal Employment Opportunity requirements.

A common approach to assessing performance is to use a numerical or scalar rating system whereby managers are asked to score an individual against a number of objectives/attributes. In some companies, employees receive assessments from their manager, peers, subordinates and customers while also performing a self assessment.

a. Personnel management
b. Human resource management
c. Progressive discipline
d. Performance appraisal

2. _____ for short is a descriptive term for certain executives in a business operation. It is also a formal title held by some business executives, most commonly in the hospitality industry.

A _____ has broad, overall responsibility for a business or organization. Whereas a manager may be responsible for one functional area, the _____ is responsible for all areas.

a. Managing director
b. Chief knowledge officer
c. Chief technology officer
d. General manager

3. A _____ is a list of the general tasks and responsibilities of a position. Typically, it also includes to whom the position reports, specifications such as the qualifications needed by the person in the job, salary range for the position, etc. A _____ is usually developed by conducting a job analysis, which includes examining the tasks and sequences of tasks necessary to perform the job.

a. Recruitment
b. Recruitment advertising
c. Job description
d. Recruitment Process Insourcing

4. In sociology, anthropology and cultural studies, a _____ is a group of people with a culture (whether distinct or hidden) which differentiates them from the larger culture to which they belong. If a particular _____ is characterized by a systematic opposition to the dominant culture, it may be described as a counterculture.

As early as 1950, David Riesman distinguished between a majority, 'which passively accepted commercially provided styles and meanings, and a '_____' which actively sought a minority style ...

a. Subculture
b. 33 Strategies of War
c. 28-hour day
d. 1990 Clean Air Act

5. _____ is the process of social and economic change whereby a human group is transformed from a pre-industrial society into an industrial one. It is a part of a wider modernization process, where social change and economic development are closely related with technological innovation, particularly with the development of large-scale energy and metallurgy production. It is the extensive organization of an economy for the purpose of manufacturing.

a. A Stake in the Outcome
b. Industrialization
c. AAAI
d. A4e

6. _____ is something that a firm can do well and that meets the following three conditions:

Competencies are things that companys execute well across several business units or product sectors.

Firms usually have few competencies, but these are usually less liable to change rapidly.

1. It provides consumer benefits
2. It is not easy for competitors to imitate
3. It can be leveraged widely to many products and markets.

A _____ can take various forms, including technical/subject matter know-how, a reliable process and/or close relationships with customers and suppliers (Mascarenhas et al. 1998.)

a. Learning-by-doing
b. NAIRU
c. Dominant Design
d. Core competency

7. _____ is the temporary suspension or permanent termination of employment of an employee or (more commonly) a group of employees for business reasons, such as the decision that certain positions are no longer necessary or a business slow-down or interruption in work. Originally the term '_____' referred exclusively to a temporary interruption in work, as when factory work cyclically falls off. However, in recent times the term can also refer to the permanent elimination of a position.
   a. Termination of employment
   b. Retirement
   c. Wrongful dismissal
   d. Layoff

8. The 'business case for _____', theorizes that in a global marketplace, a company that employs a diverse workforce (both men and women, people of many generations, people from ethnically and racially diverse backgrounds etc.) is better able to understand the demographics of the marketplace it serves and is thus better equipped to thrive in that marketplace than a company that has a more limited range of employee demographics.

An additional corollary suggests that a company that supports the _____ of its workforce can also improve employee satisfaction, productivity and retention.

   a. Virtual team
   b. Diversity
   c. Kanban
   d. Trademark

9. _____ refers to the movement of cash into or out of a business or financial product. It is usually measured during a specified, finite period of time. Measurement of _____ can be used

   - to determine a project's rate of return or value. The time of _____s into and out of projects are used as inputs in financial models such as internal rate of return, and net present value.
   - to determine problems with a business's liquidity. Being profitable does not necessarily mean being liquid. A company can fail because of a shortage of cash, even while profitable.
   - as an alternate measure of a business's profits when it is believed that accrual accounting concepts do not represent economic realities. For example, a company may be notionally profitable but generating little operational cash (as may be the case for a company that barters its products rather than selling for cash.) In such a case, the company may be deriving additional operating cash by issuing shares evaluating default risk, re-investment requirements, etc.

_____ is a generic term used differently depending on the context. It may be defined by users for their own purposes.

a. Cash flow
b. Gross profit
c. Sweat equity
d. Gross profit margin

10. _____ generally refers to a list of all planned expenses and revenues. It is a plan for saving and spending. A _____ is an important concept in microeconomics, which uses a _____ line to illustrate the trade-offs between two or more goods.
   a. 1990 Clean Air Act
   b. 33 Strategies of War
   c. Budget
   d. 28-hour day

11. _____ refers to a range of skills, tools, and techniques used to manage time when accomplishing specific tasks, projects and goals. This set encompass a wide scope of activities, and these include planning, allocating, setting goals, delegation, analysis of time spent, monitoring, organizing, scheduling, and prioritizing. Initially _____ referred to just business or work activities, but eventually the term broadened to include personal activities also.
   a. Time management
   b. Cash cow
   c. Formula for Change
   d. Voice of the customer

12. In business and accounting, _____s are everything of value that is owned by a person or company. Any property or object of value that one possesses, usually considered as applicable to the payment of one's debts is considered an _____. Simplistically stated, _____s are things of value that can be readily converted into cash.
   a. Asset
   b. AAAI
   c. A Stake in the Outcome
   d. A4e

13. _____ is a term defined by the Oxford English Dictionary as an individual's 'course or progress through life '. It is usually considered to pertain to remunerative work (and sometimes also formal education.)

The etymology of the term is somewhat ironic in that it comes from the Latin word carrera, which means race .

a. Nursing shortage
b. Spatial mismatch
c. Career planning
d. Career

14. In organizational development (or OD), the study of _____ looks at:

- how individuals manage their careers within and between organizations
- and how organizations structure the career progress of their members, it can also be tied into succession planning within some organizations.

In personal development, _____ is:

- '... the total constellation of psychological, sociological, educational, physical, economic, and chance factors that combine to influence the nature and significance of work in the total lifespan of any given individual.'

- '... the lifelong psychological and behavioral processes as well as contextual influences shaping one's career over the life span. As such, _____ involves the person's creation of a career pattern, decision-making style, integration of life roles, values expression, and life-role self concepts.'

Figures in _____

- Jeff A. Brown
- Jesse B. Davis
- Caela Farren
- John L. Holland
- Kris Magnusson
- Frank Parsons
- Vance Peavy
- Edgar Schein
- Rino Schreuder
- Mark L. Savickas
- Donald Super

a. Career development
b. Sole proprietorship
c. Business process reengineering
d. Horizontal integration

Chapter 1. Developing Managerial Competencies

15. The _____ is a United States labor law allowing an employee to take unpaid leave due to a serious health condition that makes the employee unable to perform his job or to care for a sick family member or to care for a new son or daughter (including by birth, adoption or foster care.) The bill was among the first signed into law by President Bill Clinton in his first term.

   a. Family and Medical Leave Act of 1993
   b. Sarbanes-Oxley Act of 2002
   c. Harvester Judgment
   d. Contributory negligence

16. _____ is a business management strategy, initially implemented by Motorola, that today enjoys widespread application in many sectors of industry.

   _____ seeks to improve the quality of process outputs by identifying and removing the causes of defects (errors) and variation in manufacturing and business processes. It uses a set of quality management methods, including statistical methods, and creates a special infrastructure of people within the organization ('Black Belts' etc.)

   a. Production line
   b. Takt time
   c. Theory of constraints
   d. Six Sigma

Chapter 2. Learning from the History of Management Thought 7

1. _____ is the process of social and economic change whereby a human group is transformed from a pre-industrial society into an industrial one. It is a part of a wider modernization process, where social change and economic development are closely related with technological innovation, particularly with the development of large-scale energy and metallurgy production. It is the extensive organization of an economy for the purpose of manufacturing.

   a. AAAI
   b. Industrialization
   c. A4e
   d. A Stake in the Outcome

2. A _____ or labor union is an organization of workers who have banded together to achieve common goals in key areas and working conditions. The _____, through its leadership, bargains with the employer on behalf of union members (rank and file members) and negotiates labor contracts (Collective bargaining) with employers. This may include the negotiation of wages, work rules, complaint procedures, rules governing hiring, firing and promotion of workers, benefits, workplace safety and policies.

   a. Working time
   b. Company union
   c. Labour law
   d. Trade union

3. The field of _____ looks at the relationship between management and workers, particularly groups of workers represented by a union.

   _____ is an important factor in analyzing 'varieties of capitalism', such as neocorporatism, social democracy, and neoliberalism

   a. Overtime
   b. Informal organization
   c. Organizational effectiveness
   d. Industrial relations

4. The _____ was a method of manufacturing first adopted in England at the beginning of the Industrial Revolution and later spreading abroad. Fundamentally, each worker created a separate part of the total assembly of a product, thus increasing the efficiency of factories. Workers, paid by wage, and machines were brought together in a central factory.

   a. 28-hour day
   b. 1990 Clean Air Act
   c. Factory system
   d. 33 Strategies of War

5. The sociologist Max Weber defined _____ as 'resting on devotion to the exceptional sanctity, heroism or exemplary character of an individual person, and of the normative patterns or order revealed or ordained by him.' _____ is one of three forms of authority laid out in Weber's tripartite classification of authority, the other two being traditional authority and rational-legal authority. The concept has acquired wide usage among sociologists.

In his writings about _____, Weber applies the term charisma to 'a certain quality of an individual personality, by virtue of which he is set apart from ordinary men and treated as endowed with supernatural, superhuman, or at least specifically exceptional powers or qualities.

  a. Charismatic authority
  b. 28-hour day
  c. 1990 Clean Air Act
  d. Rational-legal authority

6. _____ is a form of leadership in which the authority of an organization or a ruling regime is largely tied to legal rationality, legal legitimacy and bureaucracy. The majority of the modern states of the twentieth century are rational-legal authorities, according to those who use this form of classification.

In sociology, the concept of rational-legal domination comes from Max Weber's tripartite classification of authority; the other two forms being traditional authority and charismatic authority.

  a. Traditional authority
  b. 28-hour day
  c. 1990 Clean Air Act
  d. Rational-legal authority

7. _____ is a form of leadership in which the authority of an organization or a ruling regime is largely tied to tradition or custom. The main reason for the given state of affairs is that it 'has always been that way'.

In sociology, the concept of _____ comes from Max Weber's tripartite classification of authority, the other two forms being charismatic authority and rational-legal authority.

  a. 28-hour day
  b. 1990 Clean Air Act
  c. Rational-legal authority
  d. Traditional authority

8. _____ is a term defined by the Oxford English Dictionary as an individual's 'course or progress through life '. It is usually considered to pertain to remunerative work (and sometimes also formal education.)

Chapter 2. Learning from the History of Management Thought

The etymology of the term is somewhat ironic in that it comes from the Latin word carrera, which means race .

a. Spatial mismatch
b. Career
c. Career planning
d. Nursing shortage

9. _____ can be regarded as an outcome of mental processes (cognitive process) leading to the selection of a course of action among several alternatives. Every _____ process produces a final choice. The output can be an action or an opinion of choice.
a. Decision making
b. 1990 Clean Air Act
c. 33 Strategies of War
d. 28-hour day

10. In economics, business, retail, and accounting, a _____ is the value of money that has been used up to produce something, and hence is not available for use anymore. In economics, a _____ is an alternative that is given up as a result of a decision. In business, the _____ may be one of acquisition, in which case the amount of money expended to acquire it is counted as _____.
a. Cost overrun
b. Cost
c. Cost allocation
d. Fixed costs

11. _____ is a theory of management that analyzes and synthesizes workflows, with the objective of improving labour productivity. The core ideas of the theory were developed by Frederick Winslow Taylor in the 1880s and 1890s, and were first published in his monographs, Shop Management and The Principles of _____ Taylor believed that decisions based upon tradition and rules of thumb should be replaced by precise procedures developed after careful study of an individual at work.
a. Value engineering
b. Scientific management
c. Master production schedule
d. Capacity planning

12. A _____ is a type of bar chart that illustrates a project schedule. _____s illustrate the start and finish dates of the terminal elements and summary elements of a project. Terminal elements and summary elements comprise the work breakdown structure of the project.

a. 33 Strategies of War
b. 1990 Clean Air Act
c. 28-hour day
d. Gantt chart

13. _____ describes types of employment in which a worker is paid a fixed 'piece rate' for each unit produced or action performed. _____ is also a form of performance-related pay (PRP) and is the oldest form of performance pay.

In a manufacturing setting, the output of piece work can be measured by the number of physical items (pieces) produced, such as when a garment worker is paid per operational step completed, regardless of the time required.

a. Capacity planning
b. Methods-time measurement
c. Productivity
d. Piecework

14. In economics and sociology, an _____ is any factor (financial or non-financial) that enables or motivates a particular course of action, or counts as a reason for preferring one choice to the alternatives. It is an expectation that encourages people to behave in a certain way. Since human beings are purposeful creatures, the study of _____ structures is central to the study of all economic activity (both in terms of individual decision-making and in terms of co-operation and competition within a larger institutional structure.)

a. A Stake in the Outcome
b. A4e
c. AAAI
d. Incentive

15. The _____ is a standardized, on-scene, all-hazard incident management concept. It is a management protocol originally designed for emergency management agencies in the United States which was later federalized there. It has since been adopted by agencies in other countries.

a. A4e
b. AAAI
c. A Stake in the Outcome
d. Incident Command Structure

Chapter 2. Learning from the History of Management Thought

16. In organized labor, _____ is the method whereby workers organize together (usually in unions) to meet, converse, and negotiate upon the work conditions with their employers normally resulting in a written contract setting forth the wages, hours, and other conditions to be observed for a stipulated period. It is the practice in which union and company representatives meet to negotiate a new labor contract. In various national labor and employment law contexts, the term _____ takes on a more specific legal meaning. In a broad sense, however, it is the coming together of workers to negotiate their employment.
    a. Paid time off
    b. Collective bargaining
    c. Labour law
    d. Labor rights

17. A _____ is a list of the general tasks and responsibilities of a position. Typically, it also includes to whom the position reports, specifications such as the qualifications needed by the person in the job, salary range for the position, etc. A _____ is usually developed by conducting a job analysis, which includes examining the tasks and sequences of tasks necessary to perform the job.
    a. Recruitment advertising
    b. Recruitment Process Insourcing
    c. Recruitment
    d. Job description

18. The _____ is a form of reactivity whereby subjects improve an aspect of their behavior being experimentally measured simply in response to the fact that they are being studied, not in response to any particular experimental manipulation.

    The term was coined in 1955 by Henry A. Landsberger when analyzing older experiments from 1924-1932 at the Hawthorne Works (outside Chicago.) Hawthorne Works had commissioned a study to see if its workers would become more productive in higher or lower levels of light.

    a. 33 Strategies of War
    b. 28-hour day
    c. 1990 Clean Air Act
    d. Hawthorne effect

19. _____ refers to metrics and measures of output from production processes, per unit of input. Labor _____, for example, is typically measured as a ratio of output per labor-hour, an input. _____ may be conceived of as a metrics of the technical or engineering efficiency of production.

Chapter 2. Learning from the History of Management Thought

a. Productivity
b. Remanufacturing
c. Value engineering
d. Master production schedule

20. _____ has been described as the 'process of social influence in which one person can enlist the aid and support of others in the accomplishment of a common task' . A definition more inclusive of followers comes from Alan Keith of Genentech who said '_____ is ultimately about creating a way for people to contribute to making something extraordinary happen.'

_____ is one of the most salient aspects of the organizational context. However, defining _____ has been challenging.

a. 28-hour day
b. Situational leadership
c. Leadership
d. 1990 Clean Air Act

21. _____ is an approach to leadership development, coined and defined by Robert Greenleaf and advanced by several authors such as Stephen Covey, Peter Block, Peter Senge, Max DePree, Margaret Wheatley, Ken Blanchard, and others. Servant-leadership emphasizes the leader's role as steward of the resources (human, financial and otherwise) provided by the organization. It encourages leaders to serve others while staying focused on achieving results in line with the organization's values and integrity.
a. Affiliation
b. Adam Smith
c. Abraham Harold Maslow
d. Servant leadership

22. _____ describes the situation when output from (or information about the result of) an event or phenomenon in the past will influence the same event/phenomenon in the present or future. When an event is part of a chain of cause-and-effect that forms a circuit or loop, then the event is said to 'feed back' into itself.

_____ is also a synonym for:

- _____ signal; the information about the initial event that is the basis for subsequent modification of the event.
- _____ loop; the causal path that leads from the initial generation of the _____ signal to the subsequent modification of the event.

_____ is a mechanism, process or signal that is looped back to control a system within itself. Such a loop is called a _____ loop.

   a. Feedback loop
   b. Positive feedback
   c. Feedback
   d. 1990 Clean Air Act

23. A _____ is a name or trademark connected with a product or producer. _____s have become increasingly important components of culture and the economy, now being described as 'cultural accessories and personal philosophies'.

Some people distinguish the psychological aspect of a _____ from the experiential aspect.

   a. Brand awareness
   b. Brand extension
   c. Brand loyalty
   d. Brand

24. Some people distinguish the psychological aspect of a brand from the experiential aspect. The experiential aspect consists of the sum of all points of contact with the brand and is known as the brand experience. The psychological aspect, sometimes referred to as the _____, is a symbolic construct created within the minds of people and consists of all the information and expectations associated with a product or service.
   a. Brand awareness
   b. Channel conflict
   c. Brand management
   d. Brand image

25. In engineering and manufacturing, _____ and quality engineering are used in developing systems to ensure products or services are designed and produced to meet or exceed customer requirements. Refer to the definition by Merriam-Webster for further information . These systems are often developed in conjunction with other business and engineering disciplines using a cross-functional approach.
   a. Single Minute Exchange of Die
   b. Statistical process control
   c. Process capability
   d. Quality control

Chapter 2. Learning from the History of Management Thought

26. _____ is one of the managerial functions like planning, organizing, staffing and directing. It is an important function because it helps to check the errors and to take the corrective action so that deviation from standards are minimized and stated goals of the organization are achieved in desired manner. According to modern concepts, _____ is a foreseeing action whereas earlier concept of _____ was used only when errors were detected. _____ in management means setting standards, measuring actual performance and taking corrective action.

   a. Schedule of reinforcement
   b. Control
   c. Turnover
   d. Decision tree pruning

27. _____ is a business management strategy aimed at embedding awareness of quality in all organizational processes. _____ has been widely used in manufacturing, education, hospitals, call centers, government, and service industries, as well as NASA space and science programs.

   As defined by the International Organization for Standardization (ISO):

   '_____ is a management approach for an organization, centered on quality, based on the participation of all its members and aiming at long-term success through customer satisfaction, and benefits to all members of the organization and to society.' ISO 8402:1994

   One major aim is to reduce variation from every process so that greater consistency of effort is obtained. (Royse, D., Thyer, B., Padgett D., ' Logan T., 2006)

   a. 1990 Clean Air Act
   b. 28-hour day
   c. Total quality management
   d. Quality management

28. _____ can be considered to have three main components: quality control, quality assurance and quality improvement. _____ is focused not only on product quality, but also the means to achieve it. _____ therefore uses quality assurance and control of processes as well as products to achieve more consistent quality.

   a. 1990 Clean Air Act
   b. 28-hour day
   c. Quality management
   d. Total quality management

29. _____ is an effective method of monitoring a process through the use of control charts. Control charts enable the use of objective criteria for distinguishing background variation from events of significance based on statistical techniques. Much of its power lies in the ability to monitor both process center and its variation about that center.

Chapter 2. Learning from the History of Management Thought

a. Process capability
b. Single Minute Exchange of Die
c. Quality control
d. Statistical process control

30. _____, in strategic management and marketing is, according to Carlton O'Neal, the percentage or proportion of the total available market or market segment that is being serviced by a company. It can be expressed as a company's sales revenue (from that market) divided by the total sales revenue available in that market. It can also be expressed as a company's unit sales volume (in a market) divided by the total volume of units sold in that market.

a. Market share
b. Green marketing
c. Marketing plan
d. Business-to-business

31. _____ is the area of law in which manufacturers, distributors, suppliers, retailers, and others who make products available to the public are held responsible for the injuries those products cause.

In the United States, the claims most commonly associated with _____ are negligence, strict liability, breach of warranty, and various consumer protection claims. The majority of _____ laws are determined at the state level and vary widely from state to state.

a. Railway Labor Act
b. Product liability
c. Leave of absence
d. Right-to-work laws

32. _____ is an advertisement in which a particular product specifically mentions a competitor by name for the express purpose of showing why the competitor is inferior to the product naming it.

This should not be confused with parody advertisements, where a fictional product is being advertised for the purpose of poking fun at the particular advertisement, nor should it be confused with the use of a coined brand name for the purpose of comparing the product without actually naming an actual competitor. ('Wikipedia tastes better and is less filling than the Encyclopedia Galactica.')

In the 1980s, during what has been referred to as the cola wars, soft-drink manufacturer Pepsi ran a series of advertisements where people, caught on hidden camera, in a blind taste test, chose Pepsi over rival Coca-Cola.

a. 33 Strategies of War
b. Comparative advertising
c. 1990 Clean Air Act
d. 28-hour day

33. _____ comprises a range of practices used in an organisation to identify, create, represent, distribute and enable adoption of insights and experiences. Such insights and experiences comprise knowledge, either embodied in individuals or embedded in organisational processes or practice.

An established discipline since 1991 , _____ includes courses taught in the fields of business administration, information systems, management, and library and information sciences .

a. 1990 Clean Air Act
b. 28-hour day
c. Knowledge management
d. 33 Strategies of War

Chapter 3. Ethics and Social Responsibility

1. _____ is a contract between two parties, one being the employer and the other being the employee. An employee may be defined as: 'A person in the service of another under any contract of hire, express or implied, oral or written, where the employer has the power or right to control and direct the employee in the material details of how the work is to be performed.' Black's Law Dictionary page 471 (5th ed. 1979.)
   a. Employment counsellor
   b. Exit interview
   c. Employment rate
   d. Employment

2. The term _____ was created by President Lyndon B. Johnson when he signed Executive Order 11246 on September 24, 1965, created to prohibit federal contractors from discriminating against employees on the basis of race, sex, creed, religion, color, or national origin. In more recent times, most employers have also added sexual orientation to the list of non-discrimination.

   The Executive Order also required contractors to implement affirmative action plans to increase the participation of minorities and women in the workplace.

   a. A Stake in the Outcome
   b. A4e
   c. AAAI
   d. Equal Employment Opportunity

3. _____ is an increasingly broadening term with which an organization, or other human system describes the combination of traditionally administrative personnel functions with acquisition and application of skills, knowledge and experience, Employee Relations and resource planning at various levels. The field draws upon concepts developed in Industrial/Organizational Psychology and System Theory. _____ has at least two related interpretations depending on context. The original usage derives from political economy and economics, where it was traditionally called labor, one of four factors of production although this perspective is changing as a function of new and ongoing research into more strategic approaches at national levels. This first usage is used more in terms of '_____ development', and can go beyond just organizations to the level of nations. The more traditional usage within corporations and businesses refers to the individuals within a firm or agency, and to the portion of the organization that deals with hiring, firing, training, and other personnel issues, typically referred to as '_____ management'.
   a. Human resource management
   b. Bradford Factor
   c. Progressive discipline
   d. Human resources

4. _____ is a concept in ethics with several meanings. It is often used synonymously with such concepts as responsibility, answerability, enforcement, blameworthiness, liability and other terms associated with the expectation of account-giving. As an aspect of governance, it has been central to discussions related to problems in both the public and private (corporation) worlds.

Chapter 3. Ethics and Social Responsibility

a. Accountability
b. Usury
c. A Stake in the Outcome
d. A4e

5. _____ is a form of applied ethics that examines ethical principles and moral or ethical problems that arise in a business environment. It applies to all aspects of business conduct and is relevant to the conduct of individuals and business organizations as a whole. Applied ethics is a field of ethics that deals with ethical questions in many fields such as medical, technical, legal and _____.
   a. Facilitation payments
   b. Business Ethics
   c. Hypernorms
   d. Corporate Sustainability

6. The _____ of 2002 (Pub.L. 107-204, 116 Stat. 745, enacted July 30, 2002), also known as the Public Company Accounting Reform and Investor Protection Act of 2002 and commonly called Sarbanes-Oxley, Sarbox or SOX, is a United States federal law enacted on July 30, 2002, as a reaction to a number of major corporate and accounting scandals including those affecting Enron, Tyco International, Adelphia, Peregrine Systems and WorldCom.
   a. Fair Labor Standards Act
   b. Sarbanes-Oxley Act of 2002
   c. Letter of credit
   d. Sarbanes-Oxley Act

7. _____ is a method by which the job performance of an employee is evaluated _____ is a part of career development.

_____s are regular reviews of employee performance within organizations

Generally, the aims of a _____ are to:

- Give feedback on performance to employees.
- Identify employee training needs.
- Document criteria used to allocate organizational rewards.
- Form a basis for personnel decisions: salary increases, promotions, disciplinary actions, etc.
- Provide the opportunity for organizational diagnosis and development.
- Facilitate communication between employee and administraton
- Validate selection techniques and human resource policies to meet federal Equal Employment Opportunity requirements.

A common approach to assessing performance is to use a numerical or scalar rating system whereby managers are asked to score an individual against a number of objectives/attributes. In some companies, employees receive assessments from their manager, peers, subordinates and customers while also performing a self assessment.

a. Progressive discipline
b. Performance appraisal
c. Personnel management
d. Human resource management

8. _____ is an idea in the field of Organizational studies and management which describes the psychology, attitudes, experiences, beliefs and Values (personal and cultural values) of an organization. It has been defined as 'the specific collection of values and norms that are shared by people and groups in an organization and that control the way they interact with each other and with stakeholders outside the organization.'

This definition continues to explain organizational values also known as 'beliefs and ideas about what kinds of goals members of an organization should pursue and ideas about the appropriate kinds or standards of behavior organizational members should use to achieve these goals. From organizational values develop organizational norms, guidelines or expectations that prescribe appropriate kinds of behavior by employees in particular situations and control the behavior of organizational members towards one another.'

_____ is not the same as corporate culture.

a. Union shop
b. Organizational development
c. Organizational effectiveness
d. Organizational culture

9. A _____ or transnational corporation is a corporation or enterprise that manages production or delivers services in more than one country. It can also be referred to as an international corporation.

The first modern _____ is generally thought to be the Dutch East India Company, established in 1602.

a. Small and medium enterprises
b. Financial Accounting Standards Board
c. Command center
d. Multinational corporation

Chapter 3. Ethics and Social Responsibility

10. A _____ is a set of rules outlining the responsibilities of or proper practices for an individual or organization. Related concepts include ethical codes and honor codes.

In its 2007 International Good Practice Guidance, Defining and Developing an Effective _____ for Organizations, the International Federation of Accountants provided the following working definition:

'Principles, values, standards, or rules of behavior that guide the decisions, procedures and systems of an organization in a way that (a) contributes to the welfare of its key stakeholders, and (b) respects the rights of all constituents affected by its operations.'

   a. 1990 Clean Air Act
   b. 28-hour day
   c. 33 Strategies of War
   d. Code of Conduct

11. A _____ is a research instrument consisting of a series of questions and other prompts for the purpose of gathering information from respondents. Although they are often designed for statistical analysis of the responses, this is not always the case. The _____ was invented by Sir Francis Galton.
   a. Structured interview
   b. Mystery shoppers
   c. Questionnaire construction
   d. Questionnaire

12. A _____ occurs when an individual or organization (such as a policeman, lawyer, insurance adjuster, politician, engineer, executive, director of a corporation, medical research scientist, physician, writer, editor, or any other entrusted individual or organization) has an interest that might compromise their actions. The presence of a _____ is independent from the execution of impropriety.

In the legal profession, the duty of loyalty owed to a client prohibits an attorney (or a law firm) from representing any other party with interests adverse to those of a current client.

   a. Global Corruption Report
   b. 1990 Clean Air Act
   c. 28-hour day
   d. Conflict of interest

13. _____ is a cross-disciplinary area concerned with protecting the safety, health and welfare of people engaged in work or employment. The goal of all _____ programs is to foster a work free safe environment. As a secondary effect, it may also protect co-workers, family members, employers, customers, suppliers, nearby communities, and other members of the public who are impacted by the workplace environment.

a. AAAI
b. Occupational Safety and Health
c. A Stake in the Outcome
d. A4e

14. The _____ is the primary federal law which governs occupational health and safety in the private sector and federal government in the United States. It was enacted by Congress in 1970 and was signed by President Richard Nixon on December 29, 1970. Its main goal is to ensure that employers provide employees with an environment free from recognized hazards, such as exposure to toxic chemicals, excessive noise levels, mechanical dangers, heat or cold stress, or unsanitary conditions.

a. Unemployment Action Center
b. Occupational Safety and Health Act
c. Unemployment and Farm Relief Act
d. United States Department of Justice

15. _____ is Latin for 'Let the buyer beware'. Generally _____ is the property law doctrine that controls the sale of real property after the date of closing.

Under the doctrine of _____, the buyer could not recover from the seller for defects on the property that rendered the property unfit for ordinary purposes. The only exception was if the seller actively concealed latent defects. The modern trend in the US, however, is one of the Implied Warranty of Fitness that applies only to the sale of new residential housing by a builder-seller and the rule of _____ applies to all other sale situations.

a. 28-hour day
b. Caveat emptor
c. 1990 Clean Air Act
d. 33 Strategies of War

16. A _____ is typically described as a deliberate plan of action to guide decisions and achieve rational outcome(s.) However, the term may also be used to denote what is actually done, even though it is unplanned.

The term may apply to government, private sector organizations and groups, and individuals.

a. 1990 Clean Air Act
b. Policy
c. 33 Strategies of War
d. 28-hour day

Chapter 3. Ethics and Social Responsibility

17. The _____ 1970 is an Act of the United Kingdom Parliament which prohibits any less favourable treatment between men and women in terms of pay and conditions of employment. It came into force on 29 December 1975. The term pay is interpreted in a broad sense to include, on top of wages, things like holidays, pension rights, company perks and some kinds of bonuses.
    a. Architectural Barriers Act of 1968
    b. Oncale v. Sundowner Offshore Services
    c. Australian labour law
    d. Equal Pay Act

18. _____ is how top executives of business corporations are paid. This includes a basic salary, bonuses, shares, options and other company benefits. Over the past three decades, _____ has risen dramatically beyond the rising levels of an average worker's wage.
    a. Executive compensation
    b. Association management company
    c. Evidence-based management
    d. Anti-leadership

19. _____ is a pattern of resource use that aims to meet human needs while preserving the environment so that these needs can be met not only in the present, but also for future generations. The term was used by the Brundtland Commission which coined what has become the most often-quoted definition of _____ as development that 'meets the needs of the present without compromising the ability of future generations to meet their own needs.'

    _____ ties together concern for the carrying capacity of natural systems with the social challenges facing humanity. As early as the 1970s 'sustainability' was employed to describe an economy 'in equilibrium with basic ecological support systems.' Ecologists have pointed to the 'limits of growth' and presented the alternative of a 'steady state economy' in order to address environmental concerns.

    a. Sustainable business
    b. Sustainability reporting
    c. Global Reporting Initiative
    d. Sustainable development

20. The _____ are a set of environmental and social benchmarks for managing environmental and social issues in development project finance globally. Once adopted by banks and other financial institutions, the _____ commit the adoptees to refrain from financing projects that fail to follow the processes defined by the Principles. The _____ were developed by private sector banks - led by Citigroup, ABN AMRO, Barclays and WestLB - and were launched in June 2003.

a. Equator Principles
b. A4e
c. A Stake in the Outcome
d. AAAI

21. A mutual _____ or stockholder is an individual or company (including a corporation) that legally owns one or more shares of stock in a joint stock company. A company's _____s collectively own that company. Thus, the typical goal of such companies is to enhance _____ value.
   a. Shareholder
   b. Stockholder
   c. Free riding
   d. 1990 Clean Air Act

22. _____ is a business buzz term, which implies that the ultimate measure of a company's success is to enrich shareholders. It became popular during the 1980s, and is particularly associated with former CEO of General Electric, Jack Welch. In March 2009, Welch openly turned his back on the concept, calling _____ 'the dumbest idea in the world'.
   a. Corporate finance
   b. Shareholder value
   c. Sweat equity
   d. Gross profit margin

Chapter 4. Assessing the Environment

1. _____ is subcontracting a process, such as product design or manufacturing, to a third-party company. The decision to outsource is often made in the interest of lowering cost or making better use of time and energy costs, redirecting or conserving energy directed at the competencies of a particular business, or to make more efficient use of land, labor, capital, (information) technology and resources. _____ became part of the business lexicon during the 1980s.
   a. Operant conditioning
   b. Opinion leadership
   c. Outsourcing
   d. Unemployment insurance

2. _____ describes the relocation by a company of a business process from one country to another -- typically an operational process, such as manufacturing such as accounting. Even state governments employ _____.

   The term is in use in several distinct but closely related ways.

   a. A Stake in the Outcome
   b. AAAI
   c. Offshoring
   d. A4e

3. _____ is the use of an object (typically referred to as an RFID tag) applied to or incorporated into a product, animal, or person for the purpose of identification and tracking using radio waves. Some tags can be read from several meters away and beyond the line of sight of the reader.

   Most RFID tags contain at least two parts.

   a. Radio-frequency identification
   b. 1990 Clean Air Act
   c. 33 Strategies of War
   d. 28-hour day

4. A _____ is the system of organizations, people, technology, activities, information and resources involved in moving a product or service from supplier to customer. _____ activities transform natural resources, raw materials and components into a finished product that is delivered to the end customer. In sophisticated _____ systems, used products may re-enter the _____ at any point where residual value is recyclable.
   a. Wholesalers
   b. Drop shipping
   c. Supply chain
   d. Packaging

Chapter 4. Assessing the Environment

5. _____ is the management of a network of interconnected businesses involved in the ultimate provision of product and service packages required by end customers (Harland, 1996.) _____ spans all movement and storage of raw materials, work-in-process inventory, and finished goods from point of origin to point of consumption (supply chain.)

The definition an American professional association put forward is that _____ encompasses the planning and management of all activities involved in sourcing, procurement, conversion, and logistics management activities.

   a. Packaging
   b. Freight forwarder
   c. Drop shipping
   d. Supply chain management

6. _____ refers to the stock of skills and knowledge embodied in the ability to perform labor so as to produce economic value. It is the skills and knowledge gained by a worker through education and experience. Many early economic theories refer to it simply as labor, one of three factors of production, and consider it to be a fungible resource -- homogeneous and easily interchangeable.
   a. Market structure
   b. Deflation
   c. Productivity management
   d. Human capital

7. _____ comprises a range of practices used in an organisation to identify, create, represent, distribute and enable adoption of insights and experiences. Such insights and experiences comprise knowledge, either embodied in individuals or embedded in organisational processes or practice.

An established discipline since 1991 , _____ includes courses taught in the fields of business administration, information systems, management, and library and information sciences .

   a. 33 Strategies of War
   b. Knowledge management
   c. 1990 Clean Air Act
   d. 28-hour day

8. _____ is a type of trade policy that allows traders to act and transact without interference from government. Thus, the policy permits trading partners mutual gains from trade, with goods and services produced according to the theory of comparative advantage.

Under a _____ policy, prices are a reflection of true supply and demand, and are the sole determinant of resource allocation.

a. 28-hour day
b. 33 Strategies of War
c. 1990 Clean Air Act
d. Free Trade

9. _____ is a designated group of countries that have agreed to eliminate tariffs, quotas and preferences on most (if not all) goods and services traded between them. It can be considered the second stage of economic integration. Countries choose this kind of economic integration form if their economical structures are complementary.
   a. 33 Strategies of War
   b. 28-hour day
   c. 1990 Clean Air Act
   d. Free trade area

10. The _____ is a trilateral trade bloc in North America created by the governments of the United States, Canada, and Mexico. The agreement creating the trade bloc came into force on January 1, 1994. It superseded the Canada-United States Free Trade Agreement between the U.S. and Canada.
    a. Trade union
    b. Business war game
    c. North American Free Trade Agreement
    d. Career portfolios

11. The _____ of 1990 (ADA) is the short title of United States (Pub.L. 101-336, 104 Stat. 327, enacted July 26, 1990), codified at 42 U.S.C. § 12101 et seq. It was signed into law on July 26, 1990, by President George H. W. Bush, and later amended with changes effective January 1, 2009. The ADA is a wide-ranging civil rights law that prohibits, under certain circumstances, discrimination based on disability. It affords similar protections against discrimination to Americans with disabilities as the Civil Rights Act of 1964,
    a. Australian labour law
    b. Equal Pay Act of 1963
    c. Americans with Disabilities Act
    d. Employment discrimination

12. In economics, the people in the _____ are the suppliers of labor. The _____ is all the nonmilitary people who are employed or unemployed. In 2005, the worldwide _____ was over 3 billion people.

a. Departmentalization
b. Decent work
c. Pink-collar worker
d. Labor force

13. The _____ is the labour pool in employment. It is generally used to describe those working for a single company or industry, but can also apply to a geographic region like a city, country, state, etc. The term generally excludes the employers or management, and implies those involved in manual labour.
   a. Work-life balance
   b. Pink-collar worker
   c. Division of labour
   d. Workforce

14. _____ or _____ data refers to selected population characteristics as used in government, marketing or opinion research, or the _____ profiles used in such research. Note the distinction from the term 'demography' Commonly-used _____s include race, age, income, disabilities, mobility (in terms of travel time to work or number of vehicles available), educational attainment, home ownership, employment status, and even location.
   a. Abraham Harold Maslow
   b. Adam Smith
   c. Demographic
   d. Affiliation

15. The 'business case for _____', theorizes that in a global marketplace, a company that employs a diverse workforce (both men and women, people of many generations, people from ethnically and racially diverse backgrounds etc.) is better able to understand the demographics of the marketplace it serves and is thus better equipped to thrive in that marketplace than a company that has a more limited range of employee demographics.

An additional corollary suggests that a company that supports the _____ of its workforce can also improve employee satisfaction, productivity and retention.

   a. Virtual team
   b. Trademark
   c. Diversity
   d. Kanban

16. A _____ is a set of consistent ethic values (more specifically the personal and cultural values) and measures used for the purpose of ethical or ideological integrity. A well defined _____ is a moral code.

Fred Wenst>øp and Arild Myrmel have proposed a structure for corporate _____s that consists of three value categories. These are considered complementary and juxtaposed on the same level if illustrated graphically on for instance an organization's web page. The first value category is Core Values, which prescribe the attitude and character of an organization, and are often found in sections on Code of conduct on its web page. The philosophical antecedents of these values are Virtue ethics, which is often attributed to Aristotle. Protected Values are protected through rules, standards and certifications. They are often concerned with areas such as health, environment and safety. The third category, Created Values, is the values that stakeholders, including the shareholders expect in return for their contributions to the firm. These values are subject to trade-off by decision-makers or bargaining processes. This process is explained further in Stakeholder theory.

    a. 28-hour day
    b. 1990 Clean Air Act
    c. 33 Strategies of War
    d. Value system

17. A _____ is a research instrument consisting of a series of questions and other prompts for the purpose of gathering information from respondents. Although they are often designed for statistical analysis of the responses, this is not always the case. The _____ was invented by Sir Francis Galton.
    a. Mystery shoppers
    b. Questionnaire
    c. Structured interview
    d. Questionnaire construction

18. _____ is a term used to describe any moral, political that stresses human interdependence and the importance of a collective, rather than the importance of separate individuals. Collectivists focus on community and society, and seek to give priority to group goals over individual goals. The philosophical underpinnings of _____ are for some related to holism or organicism - the view that the whole is greater than the sum of its parts/pieces.
    a. Collaborative methods
    b. Collectivism
    c. 1990 Clean Air Act
    d. 28-hour day

19. _____ is the removal or simplification of government rules and regulations that constrain the operation of market forces. _____ does not mean elimination of laws against fraud, but eliminating or reducing government control of how business is done, thereby moving toward a more free market.

The stated rationale for '_____' is often that fewer and simpler regulations will lead to a raised level of competitiveness, therefore higher productivity, more efficiency and lower prices overall.

a. Value added
b. Natural rate of unemployment
c. Rehn-Meidner Model
d. Deregulation

20. In economics and especially in the theory of competition, _____ are obstacles in the path of a firm that make it difficult to enter a given market.

_____ are the source of a firm's pricing power - the ability of a firm to raise prices without losing all its customers.

The term refers to hindrances that an individual may face while trying to gain entrance into a profession or trade.

a. Predatory pricing
b. 28-hour day
c. 1990 Clean Air Act
d. Barriers to entry

21. _____, in microeconomics, are the cost advantages that a business obtains due to expansion. They are factors that cause a producer's average cost per unit to fall as scale is increased. _____ is a long run concept and refers to reductions in unit cost as the size of a facility, or scale, increases.
a. A4e
b. Economies of scale
c. Economies of scope
d. A Stake in the Outcome

22. The _____ is a bank regulation, which sets a framework on how banks and depository institutions must handle their capital. The categorization of assets and capital is highly standardized so that it can be risk weighted. Internationally, the Basel Committee on Banking Supervision housed at the Bank for International Settlements influence each country's banking _____ s.
a. Capital requirement
b. Reserve requirement
c. Lock box
d. 1990 Clean Air Act

23. _____ is an integrated communications-based process through which individuals and communities discover that existing and newly-identified needs and wants may be satisfied by the products and services of others.

_____ is defined by the American _____ Association as the activity, set of institutions, and processes for creating, communicating, delivering, and exchanging offerings that have value for customers, clients, partners, and society at large. The term developed from the original meaning which referred literally to going to market, as in shopping, or going to a market to buy or sell goods or services.

   a. Disruptive technology
   b. Market development
   c. Customer relationship management
   d. Marketing

24. In marketing, _____ is the process of distinguishing the differences of a product or offering from others, to make it more attractive to a particular target market. This involves differentiating it from competitors' products as well as one's own product offerings.
   a. PEST analysis
   b. Product differentiation
   c. Market development
   d. Market share

25. _____ is a concept related to the relative abilities of parties in a situation to exert influence over each other. If both parties are on an equal footing in a debate, then they will have equal _____, such as in a perfectly competitive market, or between an evenly matched monopoly and monopsony.

There are a number of fields where the concept of _____ has proven crucial to coherent analysis: game theory, labour economics, collective bargaining arrangements, diplomatic negotiations, settlement of litigation, the price of insurance, and any negotiation in general.

   a. Trade credit
   b. Buy-sell agreement
   c. 1990 Clean Air Act
   d. Bargaining power

26. _____ is an advertisement in which a particular product specifically mentions a competitor by name for the express purpose of showing why the competitor is inferior to the product naming it.

This should not be confused with parody advertisements, where a fictional product is being advertised for the purpose of poking fun at the particular advertisement, nor should it be confused with the use of a coined brand name for the purpose of comparing the product without actually naming an actual competitor. ('Wikipedia tastes better and is less filling than the Encyclopedia Galactica.')

In the 1980s, during what has been referred to as the cola wars, soft-drink manufacturer Pepsi ran a series of advertisements where people, caught on hidden camera, in a blind taste test, chose Pepsi over rival Coca-Cola.

a. 1990 Clean Air Act
b. 28-hour day
c. 33 Strategies of War
d. Comparative advertising

27. The _____ of 1968 is a United States federal law designed to protect consumers in credit transactions, by requiring clear disclosure of key terms of the lending arrangement and all costs. The statute is contained in Title I of the Consumer Credit Protection Act, as amended (15 U.S.C. § 1601 et seq.).
a. 28-hour day
b. Fair Credit Reporting Act
c. 1990 Clean Air Act
d. Truth in Lending Act

28. A _____ or labor union is an organization of workers who have banded together to achieve common goals in key areas and working conditions. The _____, through its leadership, bargains with the employer on behalf of union members (rank and file members) and negotiates labor contracts (Collective bargaining) with employers. This may include the negotiation of wages, work rules, complaint procedures, rules governing hiring, firing and promotion of workers, benefits, workplace safety and policies.
a. Labour law
b. Working time
c. Trade union
d. Company union

29. A _____ is an entity formed between two or more parties to undertake economic activity together. The parties agree to create a new entity by both contributing equity, and they then share in the revenues, expenses, and control of the enterprise. The venture can be for one specific project only, or a continuing business relationship such as the Fuji Xerox _____.
a. Patent
b. Meritor Savings Bank v. Vinson
c. Civil Rights Act of 1991
d. Joint venture

Chapter 4. Assessing the Environment

30. An _____ is a person who has possession of an enterprise and assumes significant accountability for the inherent risks and the outcome. It is an ambitious leader who combines land, labor, and capital to create and market new goods or services. The term is a loanword from French and was first defined by the Irish economist Richard Cantillon.

   a. Entrepreneur
   b. AAAI
   c. A Stake in the Outcome
   d. A4e

31. _____ generally refers to a list of all planned expenses and revenues. It is a plan for saving and spending. A _____ is an important concept in microeconomics, which uses a _____ line to illustrate the trade-offs between two or more goods.

   a. Budget
   b. 28-hour day
   c. 1990 Clean Air Act
   d. 33 Strategies of War

32. _____, in marketing, manufacturing, call centres and management, is the use of flexible computer-aided manufacturing systems to produce custom output. Those systems combine the low unit costs of mass production processes with the flexibility of individual customization.

   '_____' is the new frontier in business competition for both manufacturing and service industries.

   a. 33 Strategies of War
   b. 28-hour day
   c. 1990 Clean Air Act
   d. Mass customization

33. _____ is one of the four elements of marketing mix. An organization or set of organizations (go-betweens) involved in the process of making a product or service available for use or consumption by a consumer or business user.

   The other three parts of the marketing mix are product, pricing, and promotion.

   a. Distribution
   b. Missing completely at random
   c. Job creation programs
   d. Matching theory

Chapter 5. Managing Globally

1. In finance, the _____s between two currencies specifies how much one currency is worth in terms of the other. It is the value of a foreign nation's currency in terms of the home nation's currency. For example an _____ of 102 Japanese yen to the United States dollar means that JPY 102 is worth the same as USD 1.

   a. Exchange rate
   b. AAAI
   c. A Stake in the Outcome
   d. A4e

2. _____ is the branch of economics that studies the dynamics of exchange rates, foreign investment, and how these affect international trade. It also studies international projects, international investments and capital flows, and trade deficits. It includes the study of futures, options and currency swaps.

   a. AAAI
   b. A Stake in the Outcome
   c. A4e
   d. International finance

3. The term '_____' refers to the concept of collecting information and attempting to spot a pattern in the information. In some fields of study, the term '_____' has more formally-defined meanings.

   In project management _____ is a mathematical technique that uses historical results to predict future outcome.

   a. Regression analysis
   b. Trend analysis
   c. Least squares
   d. Stepwise regression

4. A _____ is an entity formed between two or more parties to undertake economic activity together. The parties agree to create a new entity by both contributing equity, and they then share in the revenues, expenses, and control of the enterprise. The venture can be for one specific project only, or a continuing business relationship such as the Fuji Xerox _____.

   a. Patent
   b. Civil Rights Act of 1991
   c. Meritor Savings Bank v. Vinson
   d. Joint venture

5. An _____ is a person who has possession of an enterprise and assumes significant accountability for the inherent risks and the outcome. It is an ambitious leader who combines land, labor, and capital to create and market new goods or services. The term is a loanword from French and was first defined by the Irish economist Richard Cantillon.

a. Entrepreneur
b. A Stake in the Outcome
c. AAAI
d. A4e

6. _____ is the incidence or process of transferring ownership of a business, enterprise, agency or public service from the public sector (government) to the private sector (business.) In a broader sense, _____ refers to transfer of any government function to the private sector including governmental functions like revenue collection and law enforcement.
   a. 1990 Clean Air Act
   b. Performance reports
   c. 28-hour day
   d. Privatization

7. A _____ is a set of consistent ethic values (more specifically the personal and cultural values) and measures used for the purpose of ethical or ideological integrity. A well defined _____ is a moral code.

Fred Wenst>øp and Arild Myrmel have proposed a structure for corporate _____s that consists of three value categories. These are considered complementary and juxtaposed on the same level if illustrated graphically on for instance an organization's web page. The first value category is Core Values, which prescribe the attitude and character of an organization, and are often found in sections on Code of conduct on its web page. The philosophical antecedents of these values are Virtue ethics, which is often attributed to Aristotle. Protected Values are protected through rules, standards and certifications. They are often concerned with areas such as health, environment and safety. The third category, Created Values, is the values that stakeholders, including the shareholders expect in return for their contributions to the firm. These values are subject to trade-off by decision-makers or bargaining processes. This process is explained further in Stakeholder theory.

   a. 33 Strategies of War
   b. 1990 Clean Air Act
   c. 28-hour day
   d. Value system

8. _____ is a term used to describe any moral, political that stresses human interdependence and the importance of a collective, rather than the importance of separate individuals. Collectivists focus on community and society, and seek to give priority to group goals over individual goals. The philosophical underpinnings of _____ are for some related to holism or organicism - the view that the whole is greater than the sum of its parts/pieces.

a. 28-hour day
b. Collectivism
c. Collaborative methods
d. 1990 Clean Air Act

9. In operant conditioning, _____ occurs when an event following a response causes an increase in the probability of that response occurring in the future. Response strength can be assessed by measures such as the frequency with which the response is made (for example, a pigeon may peck a key more times in the session), or the speed with which it is made (for example, a rat may run a maze faster.) The environment change contingent upon the response is called a reinforcer.
   a. Meetings, Incentives, Conferences, and Exhibitions
   b. Historiometry
   c. Diminishing Manufacturing Sources and Material Shortages
   d. Reinforcement

10. In decision theory and estimation theory, the _____ of an estimator, $\hat{\theta}$, of an unknown parameter of the distribution, θ, is the expected value of the loss function

$$R(\theta, \hat{\theta}) = \mathbb{E}_\theta L(\theta, \hat{\theta}) = \int L(\theta, \hat{\theta}) \, dP_\theta.$$

where dP_θ is a probability measure parametrized by θ.

- For a scalar parameter θ and a quadratic loss function,

$$L(\theta, \hat{\theta}) = (\theta - \hat{\theta})^2$$

the _____ function becomes the mean squared error of the estimate,

$$R(\theta, \hat{\theta}) = E_\theta(\theta - \hat{\theta})^2$$

- In density estimation, the unknown parameter is probability density itself. The loss function is typically chosen to be a norm in an appropriate function space. For example, for L^2 norm,

$$L(f, \hat{f}) = \|f - \hat{f}\|_2^2$$

the _____ function becomes the mean integrated squared error

$$R(f, \hat{f}) = E\|f - \hat{f}\|^2$$

a. Risk
b. Risk aversion
c. Financial modeling
d. Linear model

11. _____ can be regarded as an outcome of mental processes (cognitive process) leading to the selection of a course of action among several alternatives. Every _____ process produces a final choice. The output can be an action or an opinion of choice.
a. 28-hour day
b. 33 Strategies of War
c. 1990 Clean Air Act
d. Decision making

12. A _____ is a formal (explicit) agreement among firms. It is a formal organization of producers that agree to coordinate prices and production. _____ s usually occur in an oligopolistic industry, where there is a small number of sellers and usually involve homogeneous products.

a. Cartel
b. 1990 Clean Air Act
c. 33 Strategies of War
d. 28-hour day

13. A _____ or labor union is an organization of workers who have banded together to achieve common goals in key areas and working conditions. The _____, through its leadership, bargains with the employer on behalf of union members (rank and file members) and negotiates labor contracts (Collective bargaining) with employers. This may include the negotiation of wages, work rules, complaint procedures, rules governing hiring, firing and promotion of workers, benefits, workplace safety and policies.
    a. Company union
    b. Labour law
    c. Trade union
    d. Working time

14. The _____ of 1977 (15 U.S.C. §§ 78dd-1, et seq.) is a United States federal law known primarily for two of its main provisions, one that addresses accounting transparency requirements under the Securities Exchange Act of 1934 and another concerning bribery of foreign officials.
    a. Foreign Corrupt Practices Act
    b. Meritor Savings Bank v. Vinson
    c. Social Security Act of 1965
    d. Limited liability

15. _____ is a type of trade policy that allows traders to act and transact without interference from government. Thus, the policy permits trading partners mutual gains from trade, with goods and services produced according to the theory of comparative advantage.

Under a _____ policy, prices are a reflection of true supply and demand, and are the sole determinant of resource allocation.

   a. 1990 Clean Air Act
   b. 33 Strategies of War
   c. Free Trade
   d. 28-hour day

16. _____ is a designated group of countries that have agreed to eliminate tariffs, quotas and preferences on most (if not all) goods and services traded between them. It can be considered the second stage of economic integration. Countries choose this kind of economic integration form if their economical structures are complementary.

a. 33 Strategies of War
b. 28-hour day
c. 1990 Clean Air Act
d. Free trade area

17. The _____ was the outcome of the failure of negotiating governments to create the International Trade Organization (ITO.) GATT was formed in 1947 and lasted until 1994, when it was replaced by the World Trade Organization. The Bretton Woods Conference had introduced the idea for an organization to regulate trade as part of a larger plan for economic recovery after World War II.
a. Multilateral treaty
b. 1990 Clean Air Act
c. General Agreement on Tariffs and Trade
d. 28-hour day

18. The _____ is a trilateral trade bloc in North America created by the governments of the United States, Canada, and Mexico. The agreement creating the trade bloc came into force on January 1, 1994. It superseded the Canada-United States Free Trade Agreement between the U.S. and Canada.
a. Career portfolios
b. Trade union
c. Business war game
d. North American Free Trade Agreement

19. The _____ is an international organization designed by its founders to supervise and liberalize international trade. The organization officially commenced on 1 January 1995, under the Marrakesh Agreement, succeeding the 1947 General Agreement on Tariffs and Trade (GATT.)

The _____ deals with regulation of trade between participating countries; it provides a framework for negotiating and formalising trade agreements, and a dispute resolution process aimed at enforcing participants' adherence to _____ agreements which are signed by representatives of member governments and ratified by their parliaments.

a. 1990 Clean Air Act
b. Network planning and design
c. National Institute for Occupational Safety and Health
d. World Trade Organization

Chapter 5. Managing Globally

20. _____ are legal property rights over creations of the mind, both artistic and commercial, and the corresponding fields of law. Under _____ law, owners are granted certain exclusive rights to a variety of intangible assets, such as musical, literary, and artistic works; ideas, discoveries and inventions; and words, phrases, symbols, and designs. Common types of _____ include copyrights, trademarks, patents, industrial design rights and trade secrets.
   a. Intent
   b. Intellectual property
   c. Equal Pay Act
   d. Unemployment Action Center

21. A _____ or maquila is a factory that imports materials and equipment on a duty-free and tariff-free basis for assembly or manufacturing and then re-exports the assembled product, usually back to the originating country. A maquila is also referred to as a 'twin plant', or 'in-bond' industry. Nearly half a million Mexicans are employed in _____s.
   a. 33 Strategies of War
   b. 28-hour day
   c. 1990 Clean Air Act
   d. Maquiladora

22. _____ plant, and equipment, is a term used in accountancy for assets and property which cannot easily be converted into cash. This can be compared with current assets such as cash or bank accounts, which are described as liquid assets. In most cases, only tangible assets are referred to as fixed.
   a. 28-hour day
   b. Fixed asset
   c. 33 Strategies of War
   d. 1990 Clean Air Act

23. _____ is exchanging goods or services that are paid for, in whole or part, with other goods or services.

There are five main variants of _____:

- Barter: Exchange of goods or services directly for other goods or services without the use of money as means of purchase or payment.
- Switch trading: Practice in which one company sells to another its obligation to make a purchase in a given country.
- Counter purchase: Sale of goods and services to a country by a company that promises to make a future purchase of a specific product from the country.
- Buyback: occurs when a firm builds a plant in a country - or supplies technology, equipment, training, or other services to the country and agrees to take a certain percentage of the plant's output as partial payment for the contract.
- Offset: Agreement that a company will offset a hard - currency purchase of an unspecified product from that nation in the future. Agreement by one nation to buy a product from another, subject to the purchase of some or all of the components and raw materials from the buyer of the finished product, or the assembly of such product in the buyer nation.

_____ also occurs when countries lack sufficient hard currency, or when other types of market trade are impossible85 a barrel while Iraq oil sales into Asia were valued at about $22 a barrel. In 2001, India agreed to swap 1.5 million tonnes of Iraqi crude under the oil-for-food program.

a. Buy-sell agreement
b. 1990 Clean Air Act
c. Countertrade
d. Trade credit

24. _____ is exchange of capital, goods, and services across international borders or territories. In most countries, it represents a significant share of gross domestic product (GDP.) While _____ has been present throughout much of history , its economic, social, and political importance has been on the rise in recent centuries.
a. International trade
b. AAAI
c. A Stake in the Outcome
d. A4e

25. _____ refers to the methods of practicing and using another person's business philosophy. The franchisor grants the independent operator the right to distribute its products, techniques, and trademarks for a percentage of gross monthly sales and a royalty fee. Various tangibles and intangibles such as national or international advertising, training, and other support services are commonly made available by the franchisor.

a. ServiceMaster
b. 1990 Clean Air Act
c. 28-hour day
d. Franchising

26. A _____ is a formal relationship between two or more parties to pursue a set of agreed upon goals or to meet a critical business need while remaining independent organizations.

Partners may provide the _____ with resources such as products, distribution channels, manufacturing capability, project funding, capital equipment, knowledge, expertise, or intellectual property. The alliance is a cooperation or collaboration which aims for a synergy where each partner hopes that the benefits from the alliance will be greater than those from individual efforts.

a. Farmshoring
b. Process automation
c. Strategic Alliance
d. Golden parachute

27. _____s are parts of a corporation that directly add to its profit.

A _____ manager is held accountable for both revenues, and costs (expenses), and therefore, profits. What this means in terms of managerial responsibilities is that the manager has to drive the sales revenue generating activities which leads to cash inflows and at the same time control the cost (cash outflows) causing activities.

a. Factory overhead
b. Customer profitability
c. Profit center
d. Process costing

28. _____ as defined in business terms is an organization's strategic guide to globalization. A sound _____ should address these questions: what must be (versus what is) the extent of market presence in the world's major markets? How to build the necessary global presence? What must be (versus what is) the optimal locations around the world for the various value chain activities? How to run global presence into global competitive advantage?

Academic research on _____ came of age during the 1980s, including work by Michael Porter and Christopher Bartlett ' Sumantra Ghoshal. Among the forces perceived to bring about the globalization of competition were convergence in economic systems and technological change, especially in information technology, that facilitated and required the coordination of a multinational firm's strategy on a worldwide scale.

a. 1990 Clean Air Act
b. Global strategy
c. 33 Strategies of War
d. 28-hour day

Chapter 6. Fostering Entrepreneurship

1. An _____ is a person who has possession of an enterprise and assumes significant accountability for the inherent risks and the outcome. It is an ambitious leader who combines land, labor, and capital to create and market new goods or services. The term is a loanword from French and was first defined by the Irish economist Richard Cantillon.

   a. A Stake in the Outcome
   b. AAAI
   c. A4e
   d. Entrepreneur

2. A _____ is the subset of the market on which a specific product is focusing on; Therefore the market niche defines the specific product features aimed at satisfying specific market needs, as well as the price range, production quality and the demographics that is intended to impact.

   Every single product that is on sale can be defined by its _____. As of special note, the products aimed at a wide demographics audience, with the resulting low price (due to Price elasticity of demand), are said to belong to the Mainstream niche, in practice referred only as Mainstream or of high demand.

   a. Choquet integral
   b. Private placement
   c. Labor intensive
   d. Niche Market

3. _____ is the removal or simplification of government rules and regulations that constrain the operation of market forces. _____ does not mean elimination of laws against fraud, but eliminating or reducing government control of how business is done, thereby moving toward a more free market.

   The stated rationale for '_____' is often that fewer and simpler regulations will lead to a raised level of competitiveness, therefore higher productivity, more efficiency and lower prices overall.

   a. Rehn-Meidner Model
   b. Deregulation
   c. Value added
   d. Natural rate of unemployment

4. _____ according to Onuoha (2007) is the practice of starting new organizations or revitalizing mature organizations, particularly new businesses generally in response to identified opportunities. _____ is often a difficult undertaking, as a vast majority of new businesses fail. Entrepreneurial activities are substantially different depending on the type of organization that is being started.

Chapter 6. Fostering Entrepreneurship

a. AAAI
b. A4e
c. A Stake in the Outcome
d. Entrepreneurship

5. _____ are programs designed to accelerate the successful development of entrepreneurial companies through an array of business support resources and services, developed and orchestrated by incubator management and offered both in the incubator and through its network of contacts. Incubators vary in the way they deliver their services, in their organizational structure, and in the types of clients they serve. Successful completion of a business incubation program increases the likelihood that a start-up company will stay in business for the long term: Historically, 87% of incubator graduates stay in business.

a. 33 Strategies of War
b. 1990 Clean Air Act
c. 28-hour day
d. Business incubators

6. A _____ is a business that is privately owned and operated, with a small number of employees and relatively low volume of sales. The legal definition of 'small' often varies by country and industry, but is generally under 100 employees in the United States and under 50 employees in the European Union. In comparison, the definition of mid-sized business by the number of employees is generally under 500 in the U.S. and 250 for the European Union.

a. Critical Success Factor
b. Pre-determined overhead rate
c. Golden Boot Compensation
d. Small Business

7. _____ is the self-government of a nation, country or some portion thereof, generally exercising sovereignty.

The term _____ is used in contrast to subjugation, which refers to a region as a 'territory' --subject to the political and military control of an external government. The word is sometimes used in a weaker sense to contrast with hegemony, the indirect control of one nation by another, more powerful nation.

a. A4e
b. Independence
c. AAAI
d. A Stake in the Outcome

8. _____ refers to an individual's desire for significant accomplishment, mastering of skills, control, or high standards. The term was introduced by the psychologist, David McClelland.

_____ is related to the difficulty of tasks people choose to undertake.

a. Need for achievement
b. Need for power
c. 1990 Clean Air Act
d. Two-factor theory

9. A chief executive officer (_____) or chief executive is one of the highest-ranking corporate officer (executive) or administrator in charge of total management. An individual selected as President and _____ of a corporation, company, organization, or agency, reports to the board of directors. In internal communication and press releases, many companies capitalize the term and those of other high positions, even when they are not proper nouns.

a. Chief executive officer
b. Director of communications
c. Portfolio manager
d. CEO

10. The _____ is given by the United States National Institute of Standards and Technology. Through the actions of the National Productivity Advisory Committee chaired by Jack Grayson, it was established by the Malcolm Baldrige National Quality Improvement Act of 1987 - Public Law 100-107 and named for Malcolm Baldrige, who served as United States Secretary of Commerce during the Reagan administration from 1981 until his 1987 death in a rodeo accident. APQC, , organized the first White House Conference on Productivity, spearheading the creation and design of the _____ in 1987, and jointly administering the award for its first three years.

a. Business Network Transformation
b. Time and attendance
c. Scenario planning
d. Malcolm Baldrige National Quality Award

11. A _____ is a formal statement of a set of business goals, the reasons why they are believed attainable, and the plan for reaching those goals. It may also contain background information about the organization or team attempting to reach those goals.

The business goals may be defined for for-profit or for non-profit organizations.

a. Distributed management
b. Business plan
c. Time management
d. Crisis management

12. A _____ or covenant not to compete, is a term used in contract law under which one party (usually an employee) agrees to not pursue a similar profession or trade in competition against another party (usually the employer.) As a contract provision, a _____ is bound by traditional contract requirements including the consideration doctrine. The use of such clauses is premised on the possibility that upon their termination or resignation, an employee might begin working for a competitor or starting a business, and gain competitive advantage by abusing confidential information about their former employer's operations or trade secrets, or sensitive information such as customer/client lists, business practices, upcoming products, and marketing plans.

   a. Trade secret
   b. Contrat nouvelle embauche
   c. Postcautionary principle
   d. Non-compete clause

13. _____ refers to the methods of practicing and using another person's business philosophy. The franchisor grants the independent operator the right to distribute its products, techniques, and trademarks for a percentage of gross monthly sales and a royalty fee. Various tangibles and intangibles such as national or international advertising, training, and other support services are commonly made available by the franchisor.

   a. 1990 Clean Air Act
   b. ServiceMaster
   c. 28-hour day
   d. Franchising

14. A _____ is a person or investment firm that makes venture investments, and these _____s are expected to bring managerial and technical expertise as well as capital to their investments. A venture capital fund refers to a pooled investment vehicle that primarily invests the financial capital of third-party investors in enterprises that are too risky for the standard capital markets or bank loans.

   Venture capital is also associated with job creation, the knowledge economy and used as a proxy measure of innovation within an economic sector or geography.

   a. Limited liability corporation
   b. Venture capitalist
   c. Limited partners
   d. Private equity

Chapter 7. Formulating Plans and Strategies

1. _____ is an organization's process of defining its strategy and making decisions on allocating its resources to pursue this strategy, including its capital and people. Various business analysis techniques can be used in _____, including SWOT analysis (Strengths, Weaknesses, Opportunities, and Threats) and PEST analysis (Political, Economic, Social, and Technological analysis) or STEER analysis involving Socio-cultural, Technological, Economic, Ecological, and Regulatory factors and EPISTEL (Environment, Political, Informatic, Social, Technological, Economic and Legal)

_____ is the formal consideration of an organization's future course. All _____ deals with at least one of three key questions:

1. 'What do we do?'
2. 'For whom do we do it?'
3. 'How do we excel?'

In business _____, the third question is better phrased 'How can we beat or avoid competition?'. (Bradford and Duncan, page 1.)

a. Strategic planning
b. 33 Strategies of War
c. 1990 Clean Air Act
d. 28-hour day

2. The _____ is a performance management tool for measuring whether the smaller-scale operational activities of a company are aligned with its larger-scale objectives in terms of vision and strategy.

By focusing not only on financial outcomes but also on the operational, marketing and developmental inputs to these, the _____ helps provide a more comprehensive view of a business, which in turn helps organizations act in their best long-term interests. This tool is also being used to address business response to climate change and greenhouse gas emissions.

a. Commercial management
b. Middle management
c. Management development
d. Balanced scorecard

3. _____ is used to assign the available resources in an economic way. It is part of resource management.

In strategic planning,is a plan for using available resources, for example human resources, especially in the near term, to achieve goals for the future.

Chapter 7. Formulating Plans and Strategies

   a. 33 Strategies of War
   b. 1990 Clean Air Act
   c. Resource allocation
   d. 28-hour day

4. A _____ is a process in which a potential employee is evaluated by an employer for prospective employment in their company, organization and was established in the late 16th century.

A _____ typically precedes the hiring decision, and is used to evaluate the candidate. The interview is usually preceded by the evaluation of submitted résumés from interested candidates, then selecting a small number of candidates for interviews.

   a. Split shift
   b. Payrolling
   c. Supported employment
   d. Job interview

5. _____ is understood as a business unit within the overall corporate identity which is distinguishable from other business because it serves a defined external market where management can conduct strategic planning in relation to products and markets. When companies become really large, they are best thought of as being composed of a number of businesses (or _____ s.)

In the broader domain of strategic management, the phrase '_____' came into use in the 1960s, largely as a result of General Electric's many units.

   a. Switching cost
   b. Strategic drift
   c. Strategic group
   d. Strategic business unit

6. In microeconomics and strategic management, the term _____ describes a type of ownership and control. It is a strategy used by a business or corporation that seeks to sell a type of product in numerous markets. _____ in marketing is much more common than vertical integration is in production.
   a. Career development
   b. Horizontal integration
   c. Farmshoring
   d. No-bid contract

Chapter 7. Formulating Plans and Strategies

7. The _____ 1970 is an Act of the United Kingdom Parliament which prohibits any less favourable treatment between men and women in terms of pay and conditions of employment. It came into force on 29 December 1975. The term pay is interpreted in a broad sense to include, on top of wages, things like holidays, pension rights, company perks and some kinds of bonuses.
   a. Oncale v. Sundowner Offshore Services
   b. Equal Pay Act
   c. Australian labour law
   d. Architectural Barriers Act of 1968

8. _____ is how top executives of business corporations are paid. This includes a basic salary, bonuses, shares, options and other company benefits. Over the past three decades, _____ has risen dramatically beyond the rising levels of an average worker's wage.
   a. Evidence-based management
   b. Anti-leadership
   c. Association management company
   d. Executive compensation

9. The _____ of 1938 (_____, ch. 676, 52 Stat. 1060, June 25, 1938, 29 U.S.C. ch.8), also called the Wages and Hours Bill, is United States federal law that applies to employees engaged in interstate commerce or employed by an enterprise engaged in commerce or in the production of goods for commerce, unless the employer can claim an exemption from coverage. The _____ established a national minimum wage, guaranteed time and a half for overtime in certain jobs, and prohibited most employment of minors in 'oppressive child labor,' a term defined in the statute.
   a. Fair Labor Standards Act
   b. Board of directors
   c. Joint venture
   d. Family and Medical Leave Act of 1993

10. In economics and sociology, an _____ is any factor (financial or non-financial) that enables or motivates a particular course of action, or counts as a reason for preferring one choice to the alternatives. It is an expectation that encourages people to behave in a certain way. Since human beings are purposeful creatures, the study of _____ structures is central to the study of all economic activity (both in terms of individual decision-making and in terms of co-operation and competition within a larger institutional structure.)
    a. AAAI
    b. A4e
    c. A Stake in the Outcome
    d. Incentive

Chapter 7. Formulating Plans and Strategies

11. _____ are conventions, treaties and recommendations designed to eliminate unjust and inhumane labour practices. The primary inernational agency charged with developing such standards is the International Labour Organization (ILO.) Established in 1919, the ILO advocates international standards as essential for the eradication of labour conditions involving 'injustice, hardship and privation'.

   a. Anaconda Copper
   b. International labour standards
   c. Airbus SAS
   d. Airbus Industrie

12. In finance, an _____ is a contract between a buyer and a seller that gives the buyer the right--but not the obligation-- to buy or to sell a particular asset (the underlying asset) at a later day at an agreed price. In return for granting the _____, the seller collects a payment (the premium) from the buyer. A call _____ gives the buyer the right to buy the underlying asset; a put _____ gives the buyer of the _____ the right to sell the underlying asset.

   a. A Stake in the Outcome
   b. A4e
   c. AAAI
   d. Option

13. _____ is an integrated communications-based process through which individuals and communities discover that existing and newly-identified needs and wants may be satisfied by the products and services of others.

   _____ is defined by the American _____ Association as the activity, set of institutions, and processes for creating, communicating, delivering, and exchanging offerings that have value for customers, clients, partners, and society at large. The term developed from the original meaning which referred literally to going to market, as in shopping, or going to a market to buy or sell goods or services.

   a. Disruptive technology
   b. Marketing
   c. Market development
   d. Customer relationship management

14. _____ is a concept related to the relative abilities of parties in a situation to exert influence over each other. If both parties are on an equal footing in a debate, then they will have equal _____, such as in a perfectly competitive market, or between an evenly matched monopoly and monopsony.

There are a number of fields where the concept of _____ has proven crucial to coherent analysis: game theory, labour economics, collective bargaining arrangements, diplomatic negotiations, settlement of litigation, the price of insurance, and any negotiation in general.

Chapter 7. Formulating Plans and Strategies

a. Trade credit
b. Buy-sell agreement
c. 1990 Clean Air Act
d. Bargaining power

15. In economics and especially in the theory of competition, _____ are obstacles in the path of a firm that make it difficult to enter a given market.

_____ are the source of a firm's pricing power - the ability of a firm to raise prices without losing all its customers.

The term refers to hindrances that an individual may face while trying to gain entrance into a profession or trade.

a. 1990 Clean Air Act
b. Predatory pricing
c. 28-hour day
d. Barriers to entry

16. The _____ is a bank regulation, which sets a framework on how banks and depository institutions must handle their capital. The categorization of assets and capital is highly standardized so that it can be risk weighted. Internationally, the Basel Committee on Banking Supervision housed at the Bank for International Settlements influence each country's banking _____s.

a. Reserve requirement
b. Capital requirement
c. 1990 Clean Air Act
d. Lock box

17. _____ is the removal or simplification of government rules and regulations that constrain the operation of market forces. _____ does not mean elimination of laws against fraud, but eliminating or reducing government control of how business is done, thereby moving toward a more free market.

The stated rationale for '_____' is often that fewer and simpler regulations will lead to a raised level of competitiveness, therefore higher productivity, more efficiency and lower prices overall.

a. Value added
b. Deregulation
c. Natural rate of unemployment
d. Rehn-Meidner Model

Chapter 7. Formulating Plans and Strategies

18. _____, in microeconomics, are the cost advantages that a business obtains due to expansion. They are factors that cause a producer's average cost per unit to fall as scale is increased. _____ is a long run concept and refers to reductions in unit cost as the size of a facility, or scale, increases.

   a. Economies of scope
   b. A4e
   c. A Stake in the Outcome
   d. Economies of scale

19. _____ is something that a firm can do well and that meets the following three conditions:

Competencies are things that companys execute well across several business units or product sectors.

Firms usually have few competencies, but these are usually less liable to change rapidly.

   1. It provides consumer benefits
   2. It is not easy for competitors to imitate
   3. It can be leveraged widely to many products and markets.

A _____ can take various forms, including technical/subject matter know-how, a reliable process and/or close relationships with customers and suppliers (Mascarenhas et al. 1998.)

   a. NAIRU
   b. Dominant Design
   c. Learning-by-doing
   d. Core competency

20. _____ is an advertisement in which a particular product specifically mentions a competitor by name for the express purpose of showing why the competitor is inferior to the product naming it.

This should not be confused with parody advertisements, where a fictional product is being advertised for the purpose of poking fun at the particular advertisement, nor should it be confused with the use of a coined brand name for the purpose of comparing the product without actually naming an actual competitor. ('Wikipedia tastes better and is less filling than the Encyclopedia Galactica.')

In the 1980s, during what has been referred to as the cola wars, soft-drink manufacturer Pepsi ran a series of advertisements where people, caught on hidden camera, in a blind taste test, chose Pepsi over rival Coca-Cola.

Chapter 7. Formulating Plans and Strategies

a. 33 Strategies of War
b. 28-hour day
c. 1990 Clean Air Act
d. Comparative advertising

21. _____ is subcontracting a process, such as product design or manufacturing, to a third-party company. The decision to outsource is often made in the interest of lowering cost or making better use of time and energy costs, redirecting or conserving energy directed at the competencies of a particular business, or to make more efficient use of land, labor, capital, (information) technology and resources. _____ became part of the business lexicon during the 1980s.
   a. Opinion leadership
   b. Operant conditioning
   c. Unemployment insurance
   d. Outsourcing

22. _____ is one of the four growth strategies of the Product-Market Growth Matrix defined by Ansoff. _____ occurs when a company enters/penetrates a market with current products. The best way to achieve this is by gaining competitors' customers (part of their market share.)
   a. Market penetration
   b. 1990 Clean Air Act
   c. 33 Strategies of War
   d. 28-hour day

23. A _____ strategy targets non-buying customers in currently targeted segments. It also targets new customers in new segments. (Winer)

A marketing manager has to think about the following questions before implementing a _____ strategy: Is it profitable? Will it require the introduction of new or modified products? Is the customer and channel well enough researched and understood?

The marketing manager uses these four groups to give more focus to the market segment decision: existing customers, competitor customers, non-buying in current segments, new segments.

   a. Customer relationship management
   b. Product line
   c. Context analysis
   d. Market development

Chapter 7. Formulating Plans and Strategies

24. In business and engineering, new _____ is the term used to describe the complete process of bringing a new product or service to market. There are two parallel paths involved in the NProduct development process: one involves the idea generation, product design, and detail engineering; the other involves market research and marketing analysis. Companies typically see new _____ as the first stage in generating and commercializing new products within the overall strategic process of product life cycle management used to maintain or grow their market share.
    a. 28-hour day
    b. 1990 Clean Air Act
    c. 33 Strategies of War
    d. Product development

25. In economics, _____ refers to the ability of a person or a country to produce a particular good at a lower marginal cost and opportunity cost than another person or country. It is the ability to produce a product most efficiently given all the other products that could be produced. It can be contrasted with absolute advantage which refers to the ability of a person or a country to produce a particular good at a lower absolute cost than another.
    a. 33 Strategies of War
    b. 28-hour day
    c. Comparative advantage
    d. 1990 Clean Air Act

26. A _____ is the subset of the market on which a specific product is focusing on; Therefore the market niche defines the specific product features aimed at satisfying specific market needs, as well as the price range, production quality and the demographics that is intended to impact.

    Every single product that is on sale can be defined by its _____. As of special note, the products aimed at a wide demographics audience, with the resulting low price (due to Price elasticity of demand), are said to belong to the Mainstream niche, in practice referred only as Mainstream or of high demand.

    a. Private placement
    b. Niche Market
    c. Labor intensive
    d. Choquet integral

27. An _____ is a person who has possession of an enterprise and assumes significant accountability for the inherent risks and the outcome. It is an ambitious leader who combines land, labor, and capital to create and market new goods or services. The term is a loanword from French and was first defined by the Irish economist Richard Cantillon.

Chapter 7. Formulating Plans and Strategies

a. Entrepreneur
b. A Stake in the Outcome
c. AAAI
d. A4e

28. In economics, business, retail, and accounting, a _____ is the value of money that has been used up to produce something, and hence is not available for use anymore. In economics, a _____ is an alternative that is given up as a result of a decision. In business, the _____ may be one of acquisition, in which case the amount of money expended to acquire it is counted as _____.

   a. Fixed costs
   b. Cost allocation
   c. Cost
   d. Cost overrun

29. _____ is a concept developed by Michael Porter, used in business strategy. It describes a way to establish the competitive advantage. _____, in basic words, means the lowest cost of operation in the industry.

   a. Switching cost
   b. Strategic group
   c. Strategic business unit
   d. Cost leadership

30. _____ has been described as the 'process of social influence in which one person can enlist the aid and support of others in the accomplishment of a common task'. A definition more inclusive of followers comes from Alan Keith of Genentech who said '_____ is ultimately about creating a way for people to contribute to making something extraordinary happen.'

   _____ is one of the most salient aspects of the organizational context. However, defining _____ has been challenging.

   a. Leadership
   b. Situational leadership
   c. 28-hour day
   d. 1990 Clean Air Act

Chapter 8. Fundamentals of Decision Making

1. _____ can be regarded as an outcome of mental processes (cognitive process) leading to the selection of a course of action among several alternatives. Every _____ process produces a final choice. The output can be an action or an opinion of choice.

   a. 33 Strategies of War
   b. 28-hour day
   c. 1990 Clean Air Act
   d. Decision making

2. The loyalty business model is a business model used in strategic management in which company resources are employed so as to increase the loyalty of customers and other stakeholders in the expectation that corporate objectives will be met or surpassed. A typical example of this type of model is: quality of product or service leads to customer satisfaction, which leads to _____, which leads to profitability.

   Fredrick Reichheld (1996) expanded the loyalty business model beyond customers and employees.

   a. 28-hour day
   b. 33 Strategies of War
   c. 1990 Clean Air Act
   d. Customer loyalty

3. _____ is a way of expressing knowledge or belief that an event will occur or has occurred. In mathematics the concept has been given an exact meaning in _____ theory, that is used extensively in such areas of study as mathematics, statistics, finance, gambling, science, and philosophy to draw conclusions about the likelihood of potential events and the underlying mechanics of complex systems.

   The word _____ does not have a consistent direct definition.

   a. Time series analysis
   b. Statistics
   c. Standard deviation
   d. Probability

4. In decision theory and estimation theory, the _____ of an estimator, $\hat{\theta}$, of an unknown parameter of the distribution, θ, is the expected value of the loss function

$$R(\theta, \hat{\theta}) = \mathbb{E}_\theta L(\theta, \hat{\theta}) = \int L(\theta, \hat{\theta})\, dP_\theta.$$

Chapter 8. Fundamentals of Decision Making

where dP_θ is a probability measure parametrized by θ.

- For a scalar parameter θ and a quadratic loss function,

$$L(\theta, \hat{\theta}) = (\theta - \hat{\theta})^2$$

the _____ function becomes the mean squared error of the estimate,

$$R(\theta, \hat{\theta}) = E_\theta(\theta - \hat{\theta})^2$$

- In density estimation, the unknown parameter is probability density itself. The loss function is typically chosen to be a norm in an appropriate function space. For example, for L^2 norm,

$$L(f, \hat{f}) = \|f - \hat{f}\|_2^2$$

the _____ function becomes the mean integrated squared error

$$R(f, \hat{f}) = E\|f - \hat{f}\|^2$$

a. Risk aversion
b. Linear model
c. Financial modeling
d. Risk

5. A set of _____ is the verbal equivalent of a graphical decision tree, which specifies class membership based on a hierarchical sequence of (contingent) decisions. Each rule in a set of _____ therefore generally takes the form of a Horn clause wherein class membership is implied by a conjunction of contingent observations.

    IF condition$_1$ AND condition$_2$ AND ...

a. 28-hour day
b. 1990 Clean Air Act
c. Decision rules
d. 33 Strategies of War

6. In probability theory, a probability distribution is called _____ if its cumulative distribution function is _____. This is equivalent to saying that for random variables X with the distribution in question, Pr[X = a] = 0 for all real numbers a, i.e.: the probability that X attains the value a is zero, for any number a. If the distribution of X is _____ then X is called a _____ random variable.
   a. Decision tree pruning
   b. Pay Band
   c. Connectionist expert systems
   d. Continuous

7. _____ is a management process whereby delivery (customer valued) processes are constantly evaluated and improved in the light of their efficiency, effectiveness and flexibility.

Some see it as a meta process for most management systems (Business Process Management, Quality Management, Project Management). Deming saw it as part of the 'system' whereby feedback from the process and customer were evaluated against organisational goals.

   a. First-mover advantage
   b. Sole proprietorship
   c. Critical Success Factor
   d. Continuous Improvement Process

8. _____ is the discipline of managing processes in research and development (R'D) and innovation. It can be used to develop both product and organizational innovation. Without proper processes, it is not possible for R'D to be efficient; _____ includes a set of tools that allow managers and engineers to cooperate with a common understanding of goals and processes.
   a. AAAI
   b. A Stake in the Outcome
   c. A4e
   d. Innovation management

9. A _____ is a name or trademark connected with a product or producer. _____s have become increasingly important components of culture and the economy, now being described as 'cultural accessories and personal philosophies'.

Some people distinguish the psychological aspect of a _____ from the experiential aspect.

a. Brand
b. Brand awareness
c. Brand extension
d. Brand loyalty

10. _____, in marketing, consists of a consumer's commitment to repurchase or otherwise continue using the brand and can be demonstrated by repeated buying of a product or service or other positive behaviors such as word of mouth advocacy.

_____ is more than simple repurchasing, however. Customers may repurchase a brand due to situational constraints, a lack of viable alternatives, or out of convenience.

a. Brand awareness
b. Brand image
c. Brand loyalty
d. Brand extension

11. _____ is a concept based on the fact that rationality of individuals is limited by the information they have, the cognitive limitations of their minds, and the finite amount of time they have to make decisions. This contrasts with the concept of rationality as optimization. Another way to look at _____ is that, because decision-makers lack the ability and resources to arrive at the optimal solution, they instead apply their rationality only after having greatly simplified the choices available.
a. Transferable utility
b. Mixed strategy
c. Complete information
d. Bounded rationality

12. An _____ is a practitioner of accountancy, which is the measurement, disclosure or provision of assurance about financial information that helps managers, investors, tax authorities and other decision makers make resource allocation decisions.

The word '_____' is derived from the French 'Compter' which took its origin from the Latin 'Computare'. The word was formerly written in English as 'Accomptant', but in process of time the word, which was always pronounced by dropping the 'p', became gradually changed both in pronunciation and in orthography to its present form.

a. Accountant
b. A Stake in the Outcome
c. A4e
d. AAAI

13. A _____ is an alliance among individuals or groups, during which they cooperate in joint action, each in his own self-interest, joining forces together for a common cause. This alliance may be temporary or a matter of convenience. A _____ thus differs from a more formal covenant.
    a. 1990 Clean Air Act
    b. 28-hour day
    c. 33 Strategies of War
    d. Coalition

14. A _____ is a research instrument consisting of a series of questions and other prompts for the purpose of gathering information from respondents. Although they are often designed for statistical analysis of the responses, this is not always the case. The _____ was invented by Sir Francis Galton.
    a. Questionnaire construction
    b. Mystery shoppers
    c. Structured interview
    d. Questionnaire

1. _____ comprises a range of practices used in an organisation to identify, create, represent, distribute and enable adoption of insights and experiences. Such insights and experiences comprise knowledge, either embodied in individuals or embedded in organisational processes or practice.

An established discipline since 1991 , _____ includes courses taught in the fields of business administration, information systems, management, and library and information sciences .

   a. 28-hour day
   b. 33 Strategies of War
   c. Knowledge management
   d. 1990 Clean Air Act

2. A _____ is a business that is privately owned and operated, with a small number of employees and relatively low volume of sales. The legal definition of 'small' often varies by country and industry, but is generally under 100 employees in the United States and under 50 employees in the European Union. In comparison, the definition of mid-sized business by the number of employees is generally under 500 in the U.S. and 250 for the European Union.
   a. Pre-determined overhead rate
   b. Small Business
   c. Golden Boot Compensation
   d. Critical Success Factor

3. In business and accounting, _____s are everything of value that is owned by a person or company. Any property or object of value that one possesses, usually considered as applicable to the payment of one's debts is considered an _____. Simplistically stated, _____s are things of value that can be readily converted into cash.
   a. A Stake in the Outcome
   b. A4e
   c. AAAI
   d. Asset

4. _____ is a concept related to the relative abilities of parties in a situation to exert influence over each other. If both parties are on an equal footing in a debate, then they will have equal _____, such as in a perfectly competitive market, or between an evenly matched monopoly and monopsony.

There are a number of fields where the concept of _____ has proven crucial to coherent analysis: game theory, labour economics, collective bargaining arrangements, diplomatic negotiations, settlement of litigation, the price of insurance, and any negotiation in general.

Chapter 9. Using Planning and Decision Aids

   a. Trade credit
   b. 1990 Clean Air Act
   c. Bargaining power
   d. Buy-sell agreement

5. _____ is the use of an object (typically referred to as an RFID tag) applied to or incorporated into a product, animal, or person for the purpose of identification and tracking using radio waves. Some tags can be read from several meters away and beyond the line of sight of the reader.

Most RFID tags contain at least two parts.

   a. 28-hour day
   b. 1990 Clean Air Act
   c. 33 Strategies of War
   d. Radio-frequency identification

6. The _____ is the labour pool in employment. It is generally used to describe those working for a single company or industry, but can also apply to a geographic region like a city, country, state, etc. The term generally excludes the employers or management, and implies those involved in manual labour.
   a. Division of labour
   b. Workforce
   c. Pink-collar worker
   d. Work-life balance

7. _____ or _____ data refers to selected population characteristics as used in government, marketing or opinion research, or the _____ profiles used in such research. Note the distinction from the term 'demography' Commonly-used _____s include race, age, income, disabilities, mobility (in terms of travel time to work or number of vehicles available), educational attainment, home ownership, employment status, and even location.
   a. Abraham Harold Maslow
   b. Adam Smith
   c. Affiliation
   d. Demographic

Chapter 9. Using Planning and Decision Aids

8. An _____ is software that attempts to reproduce the performance of one or more human experts, most commonly in a specific problem domain, and is a traditional application and/or subfield of artificial intelligence. A wide variety of methods can be used to simulate the performance of the expert however common to most or all are 1) the creation of a so-called 'knowledgebase' which uses some knowledge representation formalism to capture the Subject Matter Experts (SME) knowledge and 2) a process of gathering that knowledge from the SME and codifying it according to the formalism, which is called knowledge engineering. _____s may or may not have learning components but a third common element is that once the system is developed it is proven by being placed in the same real world problem solving situation as the human SME, typically as an aid to human workers or a supplement to some information system.

   a. A Stake in the Outcome
   b. A4e
   c. AAAI
   d. Expert system

9. Organizational culture is not the same as _____. It is wider and deeper concepts, something that an organization 'is' rather than what it 'has' (according to Buchanan and Huczynski.)

   _____ is the total sum of the values, customs, traditions and meanings that make a company unique.

   a. Path-goal theory
   b. Job analysis
   c. Work design
   d. Corporate culture

10. The _____ is a performance management tool for measuring whether the smaller-scale operational activities of a company are aligned with its larger-scale objectives in terms of vision and strategy.

    By focusing not only on financial outcomes but also on the operational, marketing and developmental inputs to these, the _____ helps provide a more comprehensive view of a business, which in turn helps organizations act in their best long-term interests. This tool is also being used to address business response to climate change and greenhouse gas emissions.

    a. Middle management
    b. Balanced scorecard
    c. Management development
    d. Commercial management

11. In game theory, an _____ is a set of moves or strategies taken by the players, or their payoffs resulting from the actions or strategies taken by all players. The two are complementary in that given knowledge of the set of strategies of all players, the final state of the game is known, as are any relevant payoffs. In a game where chance or a random event is involved, the _____ is not known from only the set of strategies, but is only realized when the random event(s) are realized.
    a. A4e
    b. Outcome
    c. AAAI
    d. A Stake in the Outcome

12. _____ are defined as identifiable non-monetary assets that cannot be seen, touched or physically measured, which are created through time and/or effort and that are identifiable as a separate asset. There are two primary forms of intangibles - legal intangibles (such as trade secrets (e.g., customer lists), copyrights, patents, trademarks, and goodwill) and competitive intangibles (such as knowledge activities (know-how, knowledge), collaboration activities, leverage activities, and structural activities.) Legal intangibles are known under the generic term intellectual property and generate legal property rights defensible in a court of law.
    a. Interlocking directorate
    b. Induction programme
    c. Employee value proposition
    d. Intangible assets

13. _____ is the process of estimation in unknown situations. Prediction is a similar, but more general term. Both can refer to estimation of time series, cross-sectional or longitudinal data.
    a. Forecasting
    b. 33 Strategies of War
    c. 1990 Clean Air Act
    d. 28-hour day

14. The _____ is a systematic, interactive forecasting method which relies on a panel of independent experts. The carefully selected experts answer questionnaires in two or more rounds. After each round, a facilitator provides an anonymous summary of the experts' forecasts from the previous round as well as the reasons they provided for their judgments.
    a. Quality function deployment
    b. Learning organization
    c. Hoshin Kanri
    d. Delphi method

Chapter 9. Using Planning and Decision Aids 65

15. A _____ is a research instrument consisting of a series of questions and other prompts for the purpose of gathering information from respondents. Although they are often designed for statistical analysis of the responses, this is not always the case. The _____ was invented by Sir Francis Galton.
   a. Mystery shoppers
   b. Structured interview
   c. Questionnaire construction
   d. Questionnaire

16. _____ in its literal sense is the process of transformation of local or regional phenomena into global ones. It can be described as a process by which the people of the world are unified into a single society and function together.

This process is a combination of economic, technological, sociocultural and political forces.

   a. Histogram
   b. Cost Management
   c. Collaborative Planning, Forecasting and Replenishment
   d. Globalization

17. _____ is a group creativity technique designed to generate a large number of ideas for the solution of a problem. The method was first popularized in the late 1930s by Alex Faickney Osborn in a book called Applied Imagination. Osborn proposed that groups could double their creative output with _____.
   a. Affiliation
   b. Abraham Harold Maslow
   c. Adam Smith
   d. Brainstorming

18. _____ is the process of comparing the cost, cycle time, productivity, or quality of a specific process or method to another that is widely considered to be an industry standard or best practice. Essentially, _____ provides a snapshot of the performance of your business and helps you understand where you are in relation to a particular standard. The result is often a business case for making changes in order to make improvements.
   a. Competitive heterogeneity
   b. Cost leadership
   c. Complementors
   d. Benchmarking

Chapter 9. Using Planning and Decision Aids

19. Quality management can be considered to have three main components: quality control, quality assurance and _____. Quality management is focused not only on product quality, but also the means to achieve it. Quality management therefore uses quality assurance and control of processes as well as products to achieve more consistent quality.
   a. Quality improvement
   b. Quality management
   c. 28-hour day
   d. 1990 Clean Air Act

20. _____ ('Plan-Do-Check-Act') is an iterative four-step problem-solving process typically used in business process improvement. It is also known as the Deming Cycle, Shewhart cycle, Deming Wheel, or Plan-Do-Study-Act.

   _____ was made popular by Dr. W. Edwards Deming, who is considered by many to be the father of modern quality control; however it was always referred to by him as the Shewhart cycle. Later in Deming's career, he modified _____ to Plan, Do, Study, Act (PDSA) so as to better describe his recommendations.

   a. Management by exception
   b. Management team
   c. Decentralization
   d. PDCA

21. The _____ is given by the United States National Institute of Standards and Technology. Through the actions of the National Productivity Advisory Committee chaired by Jack Grayson, it was established by the Malcolm Baldrige National Quality Improvement Act of 1987 - Public Law 100-107 and named for Malcolm Baldrige, who served as United States Secretary of Commerce during the Reagan administration from 1981 until his 1987 death in a rodeo accident. APQC, , organized the first White House Conference on Productivity, spearheading the creation and design of the _____ in 1987, and jointly administering the award for its first three years.
   a. Time and attendance
   b. Business Network Transformation
   c. Malcolm Baldrige National Quality Award
   d. Scenario planning

Chapter 9. Using Planning and Decision Aids 67

22. _____ is an increasingly broadening term with which an organization, or other human system describes the combination of traditionally administrative personnel functions with acquisition and application of skills, knowledge and experience, Employee Relations and resource planning at various levels. The field draws upon concepts developed in Industrial/Organizational Psychology and System Theory. _____ has at least two related interpretations depending on context. The original usage derives from political economy and economics, where it was traditionally called labor, one of four factors of production although this perspective is changing as a function of new and ongoing research into more strategic approaches at national levels. This first usage is used more in terms of '_____ development', and can go beyond just organizations to the level of nations. The more traditional usage within corporations and businesses refers to the individuals within a firm or agency, and to the portion of the organization that deals with hiring, firing, training, and other personnel issues, typically referred to as `_____ management'.

   a. Bradford Factor
   b. Progressive discipline
   c. Human resource management
   d. Human resources

23. _____ has been described as the 'process of social influence in which one person can enlist the aid and support of others in the accomplishment of a common task'. A definition more inclusive of followers comes from Alan Keith of Genentech who said '_____ is ultimately about creating a way for people to contribute to making something extraordinary happen.'

   _____ is one of the most salient aspects of the organizational context. However, defining _____ has been challenging.

   a. 28-hour day
   b. Leadership
   c. 1990 Clean Air Act
   d. Situational leadership

24. _____ is an organization's process of defining its strategy and making decisions on allocating its resources to pursue this strategy, including its capital and people. Various business analysis techniques can be used in _____, including SWOT analysis (Strengths, Weaknesses, Opportunities, and Threats) and PEST analysis (Political, Economic, Social, and Technological analysis) or STEER analysis involving Socio-cultural, Technological, Economic, Ecological, and Regulatory factors and EPISTEL (Environment, Political, Informatic, Social, Technological, Economic and Legal)

   _____ is the formal consideration of an organization's future course. All _____ deals with at least one of three key questions:

   1. 'What do we do?'
   2. 'For whom do we do it?'
   3. 'How do we excel?'

In business _____, the third question is better phrased 'How can we beat or avoid competition?'. (Bradford and Duncan, page 1.)

   a. 1990 Clean Air Act
   b. 33 Strategies of War
   c. 28-hour day
   d. Strategic planning

25. _____ is a family of standards for quality management systems. _____ is maintained by ISO, the International Organization for Standardization and is administered by accreditation and certification bodies. The rules are updated, the time and changes in the requirements for quality, motivate change.
   a. A4e
   b. A Stake in the Outcome
   c. AAAI
   d. ISO 9000

Chapter 10. Achieving Organizational Control

1. _____ is one of the managerial functions like planning, organizing, staffing and directing. It is an important function because it helps to check the errors and to take the corrective action so that deviation from standards are minimized and stated goals of the organization are achieved in desired manner. According to modern concepts, _____ is a foreseeing action whereas earlier concept of _____ was used only when errors were detected. _____ in management means setting standards, measuring actual performance and taking corrective action.

   a. Schedule of reinforcement
   b. Decision tree pruning
   c. Turnover
   d. Control

2. _____ is the set of processes, customs, policies, laws, and institutions affecting the way a corporation (or company) is directed, administered or controlled. _____ also includes the relationships among the many stakeholders involved and the goals for which the corporation is governed. The principal stakeholders are the shareholders/members, management, and the board of directors.

   a. Flextime
   b. No-FEAR Act
   c. Corporate Governance
   d. Guarantee

3. _____ are formal records of the financial activities of a business, person, or other entity. In British English, including United Kingdom company law, _____ are often referred to as accounts, although the term _____ is also used, particularly by accountants.

   _____ provide an overview of a business or person's financial condition in both short and long term.

   a. 1990 Clean Air Act
   b. 28-hour day
   c. 33 Strategies of War
   d. Financial statements

4. _____ is a term that refers both to:

   - a formal discipline used to help appraise, or assess, the case for a project or proposal, which itself is a process known as project appraisal; and
   - an informal approach to making decisions of any kind.

   Under both definitions the process involves, whether explicitly or implicitly, weighing the total expected costs against the total expected benefits of one or more actions in order to choose the best or most profitable option. The formal process is often referred to as either CBA (_____) or BCost-benefit analysis

A hallmark of CBA is that all benefits and all costs are expressed in money terms, and are adjusted for the time value of money, so that all flows of benefits and flows of project costs over time (which tend to occur at different points in time) are expressed on a common basis in terms of their 'present value.' Closely related, but slightly different, formal techniques include Cost-effectiveness analysis, Economic impact analysis, Fiscal impact analysis and Social Return on Investment(SROI) analysis. The latter builds upon the logic of _____, but differs in that it is explicitly designed to inform the practical decision-making of enterprise managers and investors focused on optimising their social and environmental impacts.

a. Cost-benefit analysis
b. Decision engineering
c. Kepner-Tregoe
d. Gittins index

5. In accounting and auditing, _____ is defined as a process effected by an organization's structure, work and authority flows, people and management information systems, designed to help the organization accomplish specific goals or objectives. It is a means by which an organization's resources are directed, monitored, and measured. It plays an important role in preventing and detecting fraud and protecting the organization's resources, both physical (e.g., machinery and property) and intangible (e.g., reputation or intellectual property such as trademarks.)

a. Audit committee
b. Internal control
c. A Stake in the Outcome
d. Internal auditing

6. In decision theory and estimation theory, the _____ of an estimator, $\hat{\theta}$, of an unknown parameter of the distribution, θ, is the expected value of the loss function

$$R(\theta, \hat{\theta}) = \mathbb{E}_\theta L(\theta, \hat{\theta}) = \int L(\theta, \hat{\theta})\, dP_\theta.$$

where dP_θ is a probability measure parametrized by θ.

- For a scalar parameter θ and a quadratic loss function,

$$L(\theta, \hat{\theta}) = (\theta - \hat{\theta})^2$$

the _____ function becomes the mean squared error of the estimate,

$$R(\theta, \hat{\theta}) = E_\theta(\theta - \hat{\theta})^2$$

- In density estimation, the unknown parameter is probability density itself. The loss function is typically chosen to be a norm in an appropriate function space. For example, for L^2 norm,

$$L(f, \hat{f}) = \|f - \hat{f}\|_2^2$$

the _____ function becomes the mean integrated squared error

$$R(f, \hat{f}) = E\|f - \hat{f}\|^2$$

a. Financial modeling
b. Risk aversion
c. Linear model
d. Risk

7. _____ is a step in a risk management process. _____ is the determination of quantitative or qualitative value of risk related to a concrete situation and a recognized threat (also called hazard.) Quantitative _____ requires calculations of two components of risk: R, the magnitude of the potential loss L, and the probability p, that the loss will occur.
a. 1990 Clean Air Act
b. Quality assurance
c. 28-hour day
d. Risk assessment

8. _____ is the term used to describe a situation where different entities cooperate advantageously for a final outcome. Simply defined, it means that the whole is greater than the sum of the individual parts. Although the whole will be greater than each individual part, this is not the concept of _____.

Chapter 10. Achieving Organizational Control

   a. 28-hour day
   b. Synergy
   c. 33 Strategies of War
   d. 1990 Clean Air Act

9. _____ is one of a series of accounting transactions dealing with the billing of customers who owe money to a person, company or organization for goods and services that have been provided to the customer. In most business entities this is typically done by generating an invoice and mailing or electronically delivering it to the customer, who in turn must pay it within an established timeframe called credit or payment terms.

An example of a common payment term is Net 30, meaning payment is due in the amount of the invoice 30 days from the date of invoice.

   a. Accumulated Depreciation
   b. Accounts receivable
   c. A Stake in the Outcome
   d. Other revenue

10. In a human resources context, _____ or labor _____ is the rate at which an employer gains and loses employees. Simple ways to describe it are 'how long employees tend to stay' or 'the rate of traffic through the revolving door.' _____ is measured for individual companies and for their industry as a whole. If an employer is said to have a high _____ relative to its competitors, it means that employees of that company have a shorter average tenure than those of other companies in the same industry.
   a. Career portfolios
   b. Continuous
   c. Ten year occupational employment projection
   d. Turnover

11. _____ is a family of standards for quality management systems. _____ is maintained by ISO, the International Organization for Standardization and is administered by accreditation and certification bodies. The rules are updated, the time and changes in the requirements for quality, motivate change.
   a. AAAI
   b. A Stake in the Outcome
   c. A4e
   d. ISO 9000

Chapter 10. Achieving Organizational Control

12. The _____, widely known as ISO , is an international-standard-setting body composed of representatives from various national standards organizations. Founded on 23 February 1947, the organization promulgates worldwide proprietary industrial and commercial standards. It is headquartered in Geneva, Switzerland.
    a. AAAI
    b. A4e
    c. A Stake in the Outcome
    d. International Organization for Standardization

13. In game theory, an _____ is a set of moves or strategies taken by the players, or their payoffs resulting from the actions or strategies taken by all players. The two are complementary in that given knowledge of the set of strategies of all players, the final state of the game is known, as are any relevant payoffs. In a game where chance or a random event is involved, the _____ is not known from only the set of strategies, but is only realized when the random event(s) are realized.
    a. A Stake in the Outcome
    b. Outcome
    c. AAAI
    d. A4e

14. _____ refers to metrics and measures of output from production processes, per unit of input. Labor _____, for example, is typically measured as a ratio of output per labor-hour, an input. _____ may be conceived of as a metrics of the technical or engineering efficiency of production.
    a. Master production schedule
    b. Value engineering
    c. Productivity
    d. Remanufacturing

15. The _____ of 1938 (_____, ch. 676, 52 Stat. 1060, June 25, 1938, 29 U.S.C. ch.8), also called the Wages and Hours Bill, is United States federal law that applies to employees engaged in interstate commerce or employed by an enterprise engaged in commerce or in the production of goods for commerce, unless the employer can claim an exemption from coverage. The _____ established a national minimum wage, guaranteed time and a half for overtime in certain jobs, and prohibited most employment of minors in 'oppressive child labor,' a term defined in the statute.
    a. Board of directors
    b. Family and Medical Leave Act of 1993
    c. Joint venture
    d. Fair Labor Standards Act

16. In economics and sociology, an _____ is any factor (financial or non-financial) that enables or motivates a particular course of action, or counts as a reason for preferring one choice to the alternatives. It is an expectation that encourages people to behave in a certain way. Since human beings are purposeful creatures, the study of _____ structures is central to the study of all economic activity (both in terms of individual decision-making and in terms of co-operation and competition within a larger institutional structure.)

   a. Incentive
   b. A Stake in the Outcome
   c. A4e
   d. AAAI

17. _____ are conventions, treaties and recommendations designed to eliminate unjust and inhumane labour practices. The primary inernational agency charged with developing such standards is the International Labour Organization (ILO.) Established in 1919, the ILO advocates international standards as essential for the eradication of labour conditions involving 'injustice, hardship and privation'.

   a. Airbus SAS
   b. Airbus Industrie
   c. Anaconda Copper
   d. International labour standards

18. _____, when used as a special term, refers to various incentive plans introduced by businesses that provide direct or indirect payments to employees that depend on company's profitability in addition to employees' regular salary and bonuses. In publicly traded companies these plans typically amount to allocation of shares to employees.

   The _____ plans are based on predetermined economic sharing rules that define the split of gains between the company as a principal and the employee as an agent.

   a. Federal Wage System
   b. Profit sharing
   c. Wage
   d. Living wage

19. The _____ of a company or public agency is the corporate officer primarily responsible for managing the financial risks of the business or agency. This officer is also responsible for financial planning and record-keeping, as well as financial reporting to higher management. (In recent years, however, the role has expanded to encompass communicating financial performance and forecasts to the analyst community.)

Chapter 10. Achieving Organizational Control

a. 33 Strategies of War
b. 1990 Clean Air Act
c. 28-hour day
d. Chief financial officer

20. The _____ is a financial ratio that measures whether or not a firm has enough resources to pay its debts over the next 12 months. It compares a firm's current assets to its current liabilities. It is expressed as follows:

$$\text{Current ratio} = \frac{\text{Current Assets}}{\text{Current Liabilities}}$$

For example, if WXY Company's current assets are $50,000,000 and its current liabilities are $40,000,000, then its _____ would be $50,000,000 divided by $40,000,000, which equals 1.25.

a. Current ratio
b. Financial ratio
c. Times interest earned
d. Return on assets

21. In finance, a _____ or accounting ratio is a ratio of two selected numerical values taken from an enterprise's financial statements. There are many standard ratios used to try to evaluate the overall financial condition of a corporation or other organization. _____s may be used by managers within a firm, by current and potential shareholders (owners) of a firm, and by a firm's creditors.

a. Return on sales
b. Financial ratio
c. Return on equity
d. Rate of return

22. The _____ is an equation that equals the cost of goods sold divided by the average inventory. Average inventory equals beginning inventory plus ending inventory divided by 2.

The formula for _____:

The formula for average inventory:

A low turnover rate may point to overstocking, obsolescence, or deficiencies in the product line or marketing effort.

a. Asset turnover
b. Inventory turnover
c. A4e
d. A Stake in the Outcome

23. _____ is one of the Accounting Liquidity ratios, a financial ratio. This ratio measures the number of times, on average, the inventory is sold during the period. Its purpose is to measure the liquidity of the inventory.

a. Inventory
b. A Stake in the Outcome
c. Inventory turnover ratio
d. A4e

24. _____ is a concept related to the relative abilities of parties in a situation to exert influence over each other. If both parties are on an equal footing in a debate, then they will have equal _____, such as in a perfectly competitive market, or between an evenly matched monopoly and monopsony.

There are a number of fields where the concept of _____ has proven crucial to coherent analysis: game theory, labour economics, collective bargaining arrangements, diplomatic negotiations, settlement of litigation, the price of insurance, and any negotiation in general.

a. 1990 Clean Air Act
b. Trade credit
c. Buy-sell agreement
d. Bargaining power

25. A _____ is the term given to a company that facilitates the learning of its members and continuously transforms itself. _____s develop as a result of the pressures facing modern organizations and enables them to remain competitive in the business environment. A _____ has five main features; systems thinking, personal mastery, mental models, shared vision and team learning.

a. 1990 Clean Air Act
b. Hoshin Kanri
c. Quality function deployment
d. Learning organization

26. _____ is the use of control systems (such as numerical control, programmable logic control, and other industrial control systems), in concert with other applications of information technology (such as computer-aided technologies [CAD, CAM, CAx]), to control industrial machinery and processes, reducing the need for human intervention. In the scope of industrialization, _____ is a step beyond mechanization. Whereas mechanization provided human operators with machinery to assist them with the physical requirements of work, _____ greatly reduces the need for human sensory and mental requirements as well.
  a. A Stake in the Outcome
  b. AAAI
  c. A4e
  d. Automation

27. _____ generally refers to a list of all planned expenses and revenues. It is a plan for saving and spending. A _____ is an important concept in microeconomics, which uses a _____ line to illustrate the trade-offs between two or more goods.
  a. 28-hour day
  b. Budget
  c. 1990 Clean Air Act
  d. 33 Strategies of War

28. _____ is the planning process used to determine whether a firm's long term investments such as new machinery, replacement machinery, new plants, new products, and research development projects are worth pursuing. It is budget for major capital, or investment, expenditures.

Many formal methods are used in _____, including the techniques such as

- Net present value
- Profitability index
- Internal rate of return
- Modified Internal Rate of Return
- Equivalent annuity

These methods use the incremental cash flows from each potential investment, or project. Techniques based on accounting earnings and accounting rules are sometimes used - though economists consider this to be improper - such as the accounting rate of return, and 'return on investment.' Simplified and hybrid methods are used as well, such as payback period and discounted payback period.

a. Restricted stock
b. Gross profit
c. Capital budgeting
d. Gross profit margin

29. The phrase _____, according to the Organization for Economic Co-operation and Development, refers to 'creative work undertaken on a systematic basis in order to increase the stock of knowledge, including knowledge of man, culture and society, and the use of this stock of knowledge to devise new applications [sic]'

New product design and development is more than often a crucial factor in the survival of a company. In an industry that is fast changing, firms must continually revise their design and range of products. This is necessary due to continuous technology change and development as well as other competitors and the changing preference of customers.

a. Research and development
b. 1990 Clean Air Act
c. 28-hour day
d. 33 Strategies of War

30. _____ is a concept in ethics with several meanings. It is often used synonymously with such concepts as responsibility, answerability, enforcement, blameworthiness, liability and other terms associated with the expectation of account-giving. As an aspect of governance, it has been central to discussions related to problems in both the public and private (corporation) worlds.

a. A4e
b. Accountability
c. Usury
d. A Stake in the Outcome

31. An _____ is a meeting that official bodies, and associations involving the public, are often required by law to hold.

An _____ is generally held every year to inform their members of previous and future activities. It is an opportunity for the shareholders and partners to receive copies of the company's accounts as well as reviewing fiscal information for the past year and asking any questions regarding the decisions the business will take in the future.

a. A4e
b. Annual general meeting
c. A Stake in the Outcome
d. AAAI

32. An _____ is a comprehensive report on a company's activities throughout the preceding year. _____s are intended to give shareholders and other interested persons information about the company's activities and financial performance. Most jurisdictions require companies to prepare and disclose _____s, and many require the _____ to be filed at the company's registry.
   a. A Stake in the Outcome
   b. AAAI
   c. A4e
   d. Annual report

33. _____ can refer to a law of local or limited application, passed under the authority of a higher law specifying what things may be regulated by the _____, or it can refer to the internal rules of a company or organisation.

Corporate and organizational _____s regulate only the organisation to which they apply and are generally concerned with the operation of the organisation, setting out the form, manner or procedure in which a company or organisation should be run. Corporate _____s are drafted by a corporation's founders or directors under the authority of its Charter or Articles of Incorporation.

   a. Fiduciary
   b. Genuine Occupational Qualification
   c. Bylaw
   d. Racketeer Influenced and Corrupt Organizations Act

34. A _____ is a statement required of a United States firm when soliciting shareholder votes. The firm needs to file a _____ with the U.S. Securities and Exchange Commission. This statement is useful in assessing how management is paid and potential conflict-of-interest issues with auditors.
   a. 33 Strategies of War
   b. 1990 Clean Air Act
   c. Proxy statement
   d. 28-hour day

35. The _____ of 2002 (Pub.L. 107-204, 116 Stat. 745, enacted July 30, 2002), also known as the Public Company Accounting Reform and Investor Protection Act of 2002 and commonly called Sarbanes-Oxley, Sarbox or SOX, is a United States federal law enacted on July 30, 2002, as a reaction to a number of major corporate and accounting scandals including those affecting Enron, Tyco International, Adelphia, Peregrine Systems and WorldCom.
   a. Fair Labor Standards Act
   b. Sarbanes-Oxley Act of 2002
   c. Letter of credit
   d. Sarbanes-Oxley Act

36. In the fields of science, engineering, industry and statistics, _____ is the degree of closeness of a measured or calculated quantity to its actual (true) value. _____ is closely related to precision, also called reproducibility or repeatability, the degree to which further measurements or calculations show the same or similar results. _____ indicates proximity to the true value, precision to the repeatability or reproducibility of the measurement

   The results of calculations or a measurement can be accurate but not precise, precise but not accurate, neither, or both.

   a. AAAI
   b. A4e
   c. A Stake in the Outcome
   d. Accuracy

37. A chief executive officer (_____) or chief executive is one of the highest-ranking corporate officer (executive) or administrator in charge of total management. An individual selected as President and _____ of a corporation, company, organization, or agency, reports to the board of directors. In internal communication and press releases, many companies capitalize the term and those of other high positions, even when they are not proper nouns.
   a. Chief executive officer
   b. Portfolio manager
   c. CEO
   d. Director of communications

38. The _____ 1970 is an Act of the United Kingdom Parliament which prohibits any less favourable treatment between men and women in terms of pay and conditions of employment. It came into force on 29 December 1975. The term pay is interpreted in a broad sense to include, on top of wages, things like holidays, pension rights, company perks and some kinds of bonuses.

a. Equal Pay Act
b. Architectural Barriers Act of 1968
c. Oncale v. Sundowner Offshore Services
d. Australian labour law

39. _____ is how top executives of business corporations are paid. This includes a basic salary, bonuses, shares, options and other company benefits. Over the past three decades, _____ has risen dramatically beyond the rising levels of an average worker's wage.
   a. Evidence-based management
   b. Association management company
   c. Anti-leadership
   d. Executive compensation

40. The _____ duty is a legal relationship of confidence or trust between two or more parties, most commonly a _____ or trustee and a principal or beneficiary. One party, for example a corporate trust company or the trust department of a bank, holds a _____ relation or acts in a _____ capacity to another, such as one whose funds are entrusted to it for investment. In a _____ relation one person justifiably reposes confidence, good faith, reliance and trust in another whose aid, advice or protection is sought in some matter.
   a. Copyright Act of 1976
   b. Last Injurious Exposure Rule
   c. Corporate governance
   d. Fiduciary

41. _____ is used to assign the available resources in an economic way. It is part of resource management.

In strategic planning,is a plan for using available resources, for example human resources, especially in the near term, to achieve goals for the future.

   a. 28-hour day
   b. Resource allocation
   c. 33 Strategies of War
   d. 1990 Clean Air Act

42. The general definition of an _____ is an evaluation of a person, organization, system, process, project or product. _____s are performed to ascertain the validity and reliability of information; also to provide an assessment of a system's internal control. The goal of an _____ is to express an opinion on the person / organization/system (etc) in question, under evaluation based on work done on a test basis.

a. Audit
b. Internal control
c. A Stake in the Outcome
d. Audit committee

43. In a publicly-held company, an _____ is an operating committee of the Board of Directors, typically charged with oversight of financial reporting and disclosure. Committee members are drawn from members of the Company's board of directors, with a Chairperson selected from among the members. An _____ of a publicly-traded company in the United States is composed of independent and outside directors referred to as non-executive directors, at least one of which is typically a financial expert.
   a. A Stake in the Outcome
   b. Internal control
   c. Internal auditing
   d. Audit committee

44. A mutual _____ or stockholder is an individual or company (including a corporation) that legally owns one or more shares of stock in a joint stock company. A company's _____s collectively own that company. Thus, the typical goal of such companies is to enhance _____ value.
   a. 1990 Clean Air Act
   b. Stockholder
   c. Free riding
   d. Shareholder

Chapter 11. Designing Organizations

1. An _____, or organogram(me)) is a diagram that shows the structure of an organization and the relationships and relative ranks of its parts and positions/jobs. The term is also used for similar diagrams, for example ones showing the different elements of a field of knowledge or a group of languages. The French Encyclopédie had one of the first _____s of knowledge in general.
    a. AAAI
    b. A Stake in the Outcome
    c. Organizational chart
    d. A4e

2. In sociology, anthropology and cultural studies, a _____ is a group of people with a culture (whether distinct or hidden) which differentiates them from the larger culture to which they belong. If a particular _____ is characterized by a systematic opposition to the dominant culture, it may be described as a counterculture.

As early as 1950, David Riesman distinguished between a majority, 'which passively accepted commercially provided styles and meanings, and a '_____' which actively sought a minority style ...

    a. Subculture
    b. 1990 Clean Air Act
    c. 33 Strategies of War
    d. 28-hour day

3. _____ is one of the managerial functions like planning, organizing, staffing and directing. It is an important function because it helps to check the errors and to take the corrective action so that deviation from standards are minimized and stated goals of the organization are achieved in desired manner. According to modern concepts, _____ is a foreseeing action whereas earlier concept of _____ was used only when errors were detected. _____ in management means setting standards, measuring actual performance and taking corrective action.
    a. Turnover
    b. Decision tree pruning
    c. Schedule of reinforcement
    d. Control

4. _____ is a term originating in military organization theory, but now used more commonly in business management, particularly human resource management. _____ refers to the number of subordinates a supervisor has.

In the hierarchical business organization of the past it was not uncommon to see average spans of 1 to 10 or even less. That is, one manager supervised ten employees on average.

Chapter 11. Designing Organizations

a. Span of control
b. Senior management
c. Mentoring
d. CIFMS

5. _____ is a concept in ethics with several meanings. It is often used synonymously with such concepts as responsibility, answerability, enforcement, blameworthiness, liability and other terms associated with the expectation of account-giving. As an aspect of governance, it has been central to discussions related to problems in both the public and private (corporation) worlds.

a. A Stake in the Outcome
b. A4e
c. Accountability
d. Usury

6. _____ is the set of processes, customs, policies, laws, and institutions affecting the way a corporation (or company) is directed, administered or controlled. _____ also includes the relationships among the many stakeholders involved and the goals for which the corporation is governed. The principal stakeholders are the shareholders/members, management, and the board of directors.

a. Corporate governance
b. No-FEAR Act
c. Flextime
d. Guarantee

7. _____ is the process by which the activities of an organisation, particularly those regarding decision-making, become concentrated within a particular location and/or group.

a. Corner office
b. Product innovation
c. Centralization
d. Chief operating officer

8. _____ is the process of dispersing decision-making governance closer to the people or citizen. It includes the dispersal of administration or governance in sectors or areas like engineering, management science, political science, political economy, sociology and economics. _____ is also possible in the dispersal of population and employment.

Chapter 11. Designing Organizations

a. Business plan
b. Frenemy
c. Formula for Change
d. Decentralization

9. A _____ or labor union is an organization of workers who have banded together to achieve common goals in key areas and working conditions. The _____, through its leadership, bargains with the employer on behalf of union members (rank and file members) and negotiates labor contracts (Collective bargaining) with employers. This may include the negotiation of wages, work rules, complaint procedures, rules governing hiring, firing and promotion of workers, benefits, workplace safety and policies.
    a. Company union
    b. Labour law
    c. Working time
    d. Trade union

10. _____ can be defined as the idea generation, concept development, testing and manufacturing or implementation of a physical object or service. _____ers conceptualize and evaluate ideas, making them tangible through products in a more systematic approach. The role of a _____er encompasses many characteristics of the marketing manager, product manager, industrial designer and design engineer.
    a. Product design
    b. Abraham Harold Maslow
    c. Affiliation
    d. Adam Smith

11. _____ is subcontracting a process, such as product design or manufacturing, to a third-party company. The decision to outsource is often made in the interest of lowering cost or making better use of time and energy costs, redirecting or conserving energy directed at the competencies of a particular business, or to make more efficient use of land, labor, capital, (information) technology and resources. _____ became part of the business lexicon during the 1980s.
    a. Outsourcing
    b. Opinion leadership
    c. Unemployment insurance
    d. Operant conditioning

12. _____ is a dynamic of being mutually and physically responsible to and sharing a common set of principles with others. This concept differs distinctly from 'dependence' in that an interdependent relationship implies that all participants are emotionally, economically, ecologically and or morally 'interdependent.' Some people advocate freedom or independence as a sort of ultimate good; others do the same with devotion to one's family, community, or society. _____ recognizes the truth in each position and weaves them together.

a. A Stake in the Outcome
b. Interdependence
c. A4e
d. AAAI

13. A _____ is a research instrument consisting of a series of questions and other prompts for the purpose of gathering information from respondents. Although they are often designed for statistical analysis of the responses, this is not always the case. The _____ was invented by Sir Francis Galton.
   a. Mystery shoppers
   b. Structured interview
   c. Questionnaire construction
   d. Questionnaire

Chapter 12. Guiding Organizational Change and Innovation

1. _____ is a term coined by Deborah E. Meyerson used to describe corporate professionals who work toward positive change in both their work environment and the way their companies conduct business -- often taking 'radical' action that is just short of getting them fired.

In her book, _____: How Everyday Leaders Inspire Change at Work (Harvard Business School Press), Meyerson describes employees who believe and work toward creating adaptive, family-friendly, and socially responsible workplaces.

_____ are quiet leaders that act as catalysts for new ideas, alternative perspectives, and organizational learning and change -- and balance company conformity with individual rebellion.

   a. Tempered radicals
   b. 1990 Clean Air Act
   c. 33 Strategies of War
   d. 28-hour day

2. _____ is a business management strategy aimed at embedding awareness of quality in all organizational processes. _____ has been widely used in manufacturing, education, hospitals, call centers, government, and service industries, as well as NASA space and science programs.

As defined by the International Organization for Standardization (ISO):

   '_____ is a management approach for an organization, centered on quality, based on the participation of all its members and aiming at long-term success through customer satisfaction, and benefits to all members of the organization and to society.' ISO 8402:1994

One major aim is to reduce variation from every process so that greater consistency of effort is obtained. (Royse, D., Thyer, B., Padgett D., ' Logan T., 2006)

   a. 1990 Clean Air Act
   b. 28-hour day
   c. Quality management
   d. Total quality management

3. _____ can be considered to have three main components: quality control, quality assurance and quality improvement. _____ is focused not only on product quality, but also the means to achieve it. _____ therefore uses quality assurance and control of processes as well as products to achieve more consistent quality.

Chapter 12. Guiding Organizational Change and Innovation

  a. 28-hour day
  b. Total quality management
  c. Quality management
  d. 1990 Clean Air Act

4. _____ is subcontracting a process, such as product design or manufacturing, to a third-party company. The decision to outsource is often made in the interest of lowering cost or making better use of time and energy costs, redirecting or conserving energy directed at the competencies of a particular business, or to make more efficient use of land, labor, capital, (information) technology and resources. _____ became part of the business lexicon during the 1980s.
  a. Outsourcing
  b. Opinion leadership
  c. Unemployment insurance
  d. Operant conditioning

5. A _____ is a working environment with conditions that are considered by many people of industrialized nations to be difficult or dangerous, usually where the workers have few opportunities to address their situation. This can include exposure to harmful materials, hazardous situations, extreme temperatures, or abuse from employers. _____ workers often work long hours for little pay, regardless of any laws mandating overtime pay or a minimum wage.
  a. Continuous
  b. Complement
  c. Rate of return
  d. Sweatshop

6. A _____ is a set of rules outlining the responsibilities of or proper practices for an individual or organization. Related concepts include ethical codes and honor codes.

In its 2007 International Good Practice Guidance, Defining and Developing an Effective _____ for Organizations, the International Federation of Accountants provided the following working definition:

'Principles, values, standards, or rules of behavior that guide the decisions, procedures and systems of an organization in a way that (a) contributes to the welfare of its key stakeholders, and (b) respects the rights of all constituents affected by its operations.'

  a. 28-hour day
  b. 1990 Clean Air Act
  c. 33 Strategies of War
  d. Code of Conduct

Chapter 12. Guiding Organizational Change and Innovation

7. _____ is a process of gathering, analyzing, and dispensing information for tactical or strategic purposes. The _____ process entails obtaining both factual and subjective information on the business environments in which a company is operating or considering entering.

There are three ways of scanning the business environment:

- Ad-hoc scanning - Short term, infrequent examinations usually initiated by a crisis
- Regular scanning - Studies done on a regular schedule (say, once a year)
- Continuous scanning(also called continuous learning) - continuous structured data collection and processing on a broad range of environmental factors

Most commentators feel that in today's turbulent business environment the best scanning method available is continuous scanning. This allows the firm to :

-act quickly-take advantage of opportunities before competitors do-respond to environmental threats before significant damage is done

   a. AAAI
   b. A Stake in the Outcome
   c. A4e
   d. Environmental scanning

8. In the field of Organizational Development there are many activities and disciplines. One of those is the area of _____ and the use of structured organizational diagnostic tools.

The effective diagnosis of organizational culture, and structural and operational strengths and weaknesses are fundamental to any successful organizational development intervention.

   a. AAAI
   b. A4e
   c. A Stake in the Outcome
   d. Organizational diagnosis

9. In sociology, anthropology and cultural studies, a _____ is a group of people with a culture (whether distinct or hidden) which differentiates them from the larger culture to which they belong. If a particular _____ is characterized by a systematic opposition to the dominant culture, it may be described as a counterculture.

As early as 1950, David Riesman distinguished between a majority, 'which passively accepted commercially provided styles and meanings, and a '_____' which actively sought a minority style ...

a. 33 Strategies of War
b. 1990 Clean Air Act
c. 28-hour day
d. Subculture

10. The _____ is a performance management tool for measuring whether the smaller-scale operational activities of a company are aligned with its larger-scale objectives in terms of vision and strategy.

By focusing not only on financial outcomes but also on the operational, marketing and developmental inputs to these, the _____ helps provide a more comprehensive view of a business, which in turn helps organizations act in their best long-term interests. This tool is also being used to address business response to climate change and greenhouse gas emissions.

a. Commercial management
b. Management development
c. Middle management
d. Balanced scorecard

11. _____ is the temporary suspension or permanent termination of employment of an employee or (more commonly) a group of employees for business reasons, such as the decision that certain positions are no longer necessary or a business slow-down or interruption in work. Originally the term '_____' referred exclusively to a temporary interruption in work, as when factory work cyclically falls off. However, in recent times the term can also refer to the permanent elimination of a position.
a. Wrongful dismissal
b. Termination of employment
c. Layoff
d. Retirement

12. _____ is a structured approach to transitioning individuals, teams, and organizations from a current state to a desired future state. The current definition of _____ includes both organizational _____ processes and individual _____ models, which together are used to manage the people side of change.

A number of models are available for understanding the transitioning of individuals through the phases of _____ and strengthening organizational development initiative in both government and corporate sectors.

Chapter 12. Guiding Organizational Change and Innovation

a. 1990 Clean Air Act
b. 28-hour day
c. Change management
d. 33 Strategies of War

13. _____ is the corporate management term for the act of reorganizing the legal, ownership, operational, or other structures of a company for the purpose of making it more profitable, or better organized for its present needs. Alternate reasons for _____ include a change of ownership or ownership structure, demerger repositioning debt _____ and financial _____.
   a. Market value added
   b. Net worth
   c. Market value
   d. Restructuring

14. In mathematical logic, _____ is a valid argument and rule of inference which makes the inference that, if the conjunction A and B is true, then A is true, and B is true.

In formal language:

$$A \wedge B \vdash A$$

or

$$A \wedge B \vdash B$$

The argument has one premise, namely a conjunction, and one often uses _____ in longer arguments to derive one of the conjuncts.

An example in English:

It's raining and it's pouring.

a. Simplification
b. 1990 Clean Air Act
c. Validity
d. Fuzzy logic

15. A _____ is a form of qualitative research in which a group of people are asked about their attitude towards a product, service, concept, advertisement, idea, or packaging. Questions are asked in an interactive group setting where participants are free to talk with other group members.

The first _____s were created at the Bureau of Applied Social Research by associate director, sociologist Robert K. Merton.

   a. Marketing research
   b. Market analysis
   c. 1990 Clean Air Act
   d. Focus group

16. _____ is an attempt to motivate employees by giving them the opportunity to use the range of their abilities. It is an idea that was developed by the American psychologist Frederick Herzberg in the 1950s. It can be contrasted to job enlargement which simply increases the number of tasks without changing the challenge.
   a. C-A-K-E
   b. Cash cow
   c. Job enrichment
   d. Catfish effect

17. _____. The objective of OD is to improve the organization's capacity to handle its internal and external functioning and relationships. This would include such things as improved interpersonal and group processes, more effective communication, enhanced ability to cope with organizational problems of all kinds, more effective decision processes, more appropriate leadership style, improved skill in dealing with destructive conflict, and higher levels of trust and cooperation among organizational members.
   a. Organizational structure
   b. Organizational development
   c. Industrial relations
   d. Improved Organizational Performance

18. A _____ is a research instrument consisting of a series of questions and other prompts for the purpose of gathering information from respondents. Although they are often designed for statistical analysis of the responses, this is not always the case. The _____ was invented by Sir Francis Galton.
   a. Mystery shoppers
   b. Structured interview
   c. Questionnaire construction
   d. Questionnaire

Chapter 12. Guiding Organizational Change and Innovation

19. _____ describes the situation when output from (or information about the result of) an event or phenomenon in the past will influence the same event/phenomenon in the present or future. When an event is part of a chain of cause-and-effect that forms a circuit or loop, then the event is said to 'feed back' into itself.

_____ is also a synonym for:

- _____ signal; the information about the initial event that is the basis for subsequent modification of the event.
- _____ loop; the causal path that leads from the initial generation of the _____ signal to the subsequent modification of the event.

_____ is a mechanism, process or signal that is looped back to control a system within itself. Such a loop is called a _____ loop.

 a. Feedback loop
 b. Positive feedback
 c. 1990 Clean Air Act
 d. Feedback

20. _____ is a company-wide computer software system used to manage and coordinate all the resources, information, and functions of a business from shared data stores.

An _____ system has a service-oriented architecture with modular hardware and software units and 'services' that communicate on a local area network. The modular design allows a business to add or reconfigure modules (perhaps from different vendors) while preserving data integrity in one shared database that may be centralized or distributed.

 a. Enterprise resource planning
 b. A Stake in the Outcome
 c. AAAI
 d. A4e

21. A _____ is the term given to a company that facilitates the learning of its members and continuously transforms itself. _____s develop as a result of the pressures facing modern organizations and enables them to remain competitive in the business environment. A _____ has five main features; systems thinking, personal mastery, mental models, shared vision and team learning.

Chapter 12. Guiding Organizational Change and Innovation

a. Quality function deployment
b. 1990 Clean Air Act
c. Learning organization
d. Hoshin Kanri

22. _____ has been described as the 'process of social influence in which one person can enlist the aid and support of others in the accomplishment of a common task'. A definition more inclusive of followers comes from Alan Keith of Genentech who said '_____ is ultimately about creating a way for people to contribute to making something extraordinary happen.'

_____ is one of the most salient aspects of the organizational context. However, defining _____ has been challenging.

a. 1990 Clean Air Act
b. 28-hour day
c. Situational leadership
d. Leadership

23. _____ refers to increasing the spiritual, political, social or economic strength of individuals and communities. It often involves the empowered developing confidence in their own capacities.

The term Human _____ covers a vast landscape of meanings, interpretations, definitions and disciplines ranging from psychology and philosophy to the highly commercialized Self-Help industry and Motivational sciences.

a. Empowerment
b. AAAI
c. A Stake in the Outcome
d. A4e

24. In probability theory, a probability distribution is called _____ if its cumulative distribution function is _____. This is equivalent to saying that for random variables X with the distribution in question, Pr[X = a] = 0 for all real numbers a, i.e.: the probability that X attains the value a is zero, for any number a. If the distribution of X is _____ then X is called a _____ random variable.
a. Pay Band
b. Decision tree pruning
c. Continuous
d. Connectionist expert systems

25. _____ is a concept related to the relative abilities of parties in a situation to exert influence over each other. If both parties are on an equal footing in a debate, then they will have equal _____, such as in a perfectly competitive market, or between an evenly matched monopoly and monopsony.

There are a number of fields where the concept of _____ has proven crucial to coherent analysis: game theory, labour economics, collective bargaining arrangements, diplomatic negotiations, settlement of litigation, the price of insurance, and any negotiation in general.

a. Trade credit
b. Buy-sell agreement
c. Bargaining power
d. 1990 Clean Air Act

26. _____ is a subfield of the larger discipline of communication studies. _____, as a field, is the consideration, analysis, and criticism of the role of communication in organizational contexts.

The field traces its lineage through business information, business communication, and early mass communication studies published in the 1930s through the 1950s.

a. AAAI
b. A4e
c. A Stake in the Outcome
d. Organizational communication

27. In business and accounting, _____s are everything of value that is owned by a person or company. Any property or object of value that one possesses, usually considered as applicable to the payment of one's debts is considered an _____. Simplistically stated, _____s are things of value that can be readily converted into cash.

a. A4e
b. AAAI
c. A Stake in the Outcome
d. Asset

Chapter 13. Managing Human Resources

1. _____ is an increasingly broadening term with which an organization, or other human system describes the combination of traditionally administrative personnel functions with acquisition and application of skills, knowledge and experience, Employee Relations and resource planning at various levels. The field draws upon concepts developed in Industrial/Organizational Psychology and System Theory. _____ has at least two related interpretations depending on context. The original usage derives from political economy and economics, where it was traditionally called labor, one of four factors of production although this perspective is changing as a function of new and ongoing research into more strategic approaches at national levels. This first usage is used more in terms of '_____ development', and can go beyond just organizations to the level of nations . The more traditional usage within corporations and businesses refers to the individuals within a firm or agency, and to the portion of the organization that deals with hiring, firing, training, and other personnel issues, typically referred to as `_____ management'.
    a. Human resource management
    b. Bradford Factor
    c. Human resources
    d. Progressive discipline

2. _____ is, in very basic words, a position a firm occupies against its competitors.

According to Michael Porter, the three methods for creating a sustainable _____ are through:

1. Cost leadership

2. Differentiation

3. Focus (economics)

    a. Competitive advantage
    b. 28-hour day
    c. Theory Z
    d. 1990 Clean Air Act

3. _____ is a contract between two parties, one being the employer and the other being the employee. An employee may be defined as: 'A person in the service of another under any contract of hire, express or implied, oral or written, where the employer has the power or right to control and direct the employee in the material details of how the work is to be performed.' Black's Law Dictionary page 471 (5th ed. 1979.)
    a. Employment rate
    b. Exit interview
    c. Employment
    d. Employment counsellor

Chapter 13. Managing Human Resources

4. _____ is the body of laws, administrative rulings, and precedents which address the legal rights of, and restrictions on, working people and their organizations. As such, it mediates many aspects of the relationship between trade unions, employers and employees. In Canada, employment laws related to unionized workplaces are differentiated from those relating to particular individuals.
   a. Trade union
   b. Shift work
   c. Four-day week
   d. Labor law

5. The term _____ was created by President Lyndon B. Johnson when he signed Executive Order 11246 on September 24, 1965, created to prohibit federal contractors from discriminating against employees on the basis of race, sex, creed, religion, color, or national origin. In more recent times, most employers have also added sexual orientation to the list of non-discrimination.

The Executive Order also required contractors to implement affirmative action plans to increase the participation of minorities and women in the workplace.

   a. AAAI
   b. A4e
   c. A Stake in the Outcome
   d. Equal Employment Opportunity

6. The _____ of 1967, Pub. L. No. 90-202, 81 Stat. 602 (Dec. 15, 1967), codified as Chapter 14 of Title 29 of the United States Code, 29 U.S.C. § 621 through 29 U.S.C. § 634 (ADEA), prohibits employment discrimination against persons 40 years of age or older in the United States). The law also sets standards for pensions and benefits provided by employers and requires that information about the needs of older workers be provided to the general public.
   a. Age Discrimination in Employment Act
   b. Undue hardship
   c. Extra time
   d. Unemployment and Farm Relief Act

7. The _____ of 1990 (ADA) is the short title of United States (Pub.L. 101-336, 104 Stat. 327, enacted July 26, 1990), codified at 42 U.S.C. § 12101 et seq. It was signed into law on July 26, 1990, by President George H. W. Bush, and later amended with changes effective January 1, 2009. The ADA is a wide-ranging civil rights law that prohibits, under certain circumstances, discrimination based on disability. It affords similar protections against discrimination to Americans with disabilities as the Civil Rights Act of 1964,

Chapter 13. Managing Human Resources

a. Employment discrimination
b. Americans with Disabilities Act
c. Equal Pay Act of 1963
d. Australian labour law

8. The _____ 1970 is an Act of the United Kingdom Parliament which prohibits any less favourable treatment between men and women in terms of pay and conditions of employment. It came into force on 29 December 1975. The term pay is interpreted in a broad sense to include, on top of wages, things like holidays, pension rights, company perks and some kinds of bonuses.
    a. Australian labour law
    b. Oncale v. Sundowner Offshore Services
    c. Equal Pay Act
    d. Architectural Barriers Act of 1968

9. The _____ of 1938 (_____, ch. 676, 52 Stat. 1060, June 25, 1938, 29 U.S.C. ch.8), also called the Wages and Hours Bill, is United States federal law that applies to employees engaged in interstate commerce or employed by an enterprise engaged in commerce or in the production of goods for commerce, unless the employer can claim an exemption from coverage. The _____ established a national minimum wage, guaranteed time and a half for overtime in certain jobs, and prohibited most employment of minors in 'oppressive child labor,' a term defined in the statute.
    a. Family and Medical Leave Act of 1993
    b. Joint venture
    c. Board of directors
    d. Fair Labor Standards Act

10. The _____ is a United States labor law allowing an employee to take unpaid leave due to a serious health condition that makes the employee unable to perform his job or to care for a sick family member or to care for a new son or daughter (including by birth, adoption or foster care.) The bill was among the first signed into law by President Bill Clinton in his first term.
    a. Sarbanes-Oxley Act of 2002
    b. Family and Medical Leave Act of 1993
    c. Contributory negligence
    d. Harvester Judgment

11. The field of _____ looks at the relationship between management and workers, particularly groups of workers represented by a union.

_____ is an important factor in analyzing 'varieties of capitalism', such as neocorporatism, social democracy, and neoliberalism

a. Overtime
b. Informal organization
c. Organizational effectiveness
d. Industrial relations

12. _____ are conventions, treaties and recommendations designed to eliminate unjust and inhumane labour practices. The primary inernational agency charged with developing such standards is the International Labour Organization (ILO.) Established in 1919, the ILO advocates international standards as essential for the eradication of labour conditions involving 'injustice, hardship and privation'.
a. Airbus SAS
b. Airbus Industrie
c. Anaconda Copper
d. International labour standards

13. The _____ is a 1935 United States federal law that limits the means with which employers may react to workers in the private sector that organize labor unions, engage in collective bargaining, and take part in strikes and other forms of concerted activity in support of their demands. The Act does not, on the other hand, cover those workers who are covered by the Railway Labor Act, agricultural employees, domestic employees, supervisors, independent contractors and some close relatives of individual employers.

It was in a context of severe economic troubles that the Wagner Act came into effect.

a. 1990 Clean Air Act
b. 28-hour day
c. 33 Strategies of War
d. National Labor Relations Act

14. _____ is a cross-disciplinary area concerned with protecting the safety, health and welfare of people engaged in work or employment. The goal of all _____ programs is to foster a work free safe environment. As a secondary effect, it may also protect co-workers, family members, employers, customers, suppliers, nearby communities, and other members of the public who are impacted by the workplace environment.
a. AAAI
b. A Stake in the Outcome
c. A4e
d. Occupational Safety and Health

15. The _____ is the primary federal law which governs occupational health and safety in the private sector and federal government in the United States. It was enacted by Congress in 1970 and was signed by President Richard Nixon on December 29, 1970. Its main goal is to ensure that employers provide employees with an environment free from recognized hazards, such as exposure to toxic chemicals, excessive noise levels, mechanical dangers, heat or cold stress, or unsanitary conditions.
   a. United States Department of Justice
   b. Occupational Safety and Health Act
   c. Unemployment and Farm Relief Act
   d. Unemployment Action Center

16. _____ occurs when expectant women are fired, not hired, or otherwise discriminated against due to their pregnancy or intention to become pregnant. Common forms of _____ include not being hired due to visible pregnancy or likelihood of becoming pregnant, being fired after informing an employer of one's pregnancy, being fired after maternity leave, and receiving a pay dock due to pregnancy. In the United States, since 1978, employers are legally bound to provide what insurance, leave pay, and additional support that would be bestowed upon any employee with medical leave or disability.
   a. 28-hour day
   b. Pregnancy Discrimination
   c. 1990 Clean Air Act
   d. 33 Strategies of War

17. _____ is the process of learning a new skill or trade, often in response to a change in the economic environment. Generally it reflects changes in profession choice rather than an 'upward' movement in the same field.

There is some controversy surrounding the use of _____ to offset economic changes caused by free trade and automation.

   a. Compliance Training
   b. Suspension training
   c. Krauthammer
   d. Retraining

18. The _____ is a United States labor law which protects employees, their families, and communities by requiring most employers with 100 or more employees to provide sixty- (60) calendar-day advance notification of plant closings and mass layoffs of employees. It was enacted in 1989.

Employees entitled to notice under the _____ include managers and supervisors, hourly wage, and salaried workers.

Chapter 13. Managing Human Resources

a. Robinson-Patman Act
b. Worker Adjustment and Retraining Notification Act
c. Leave of absence
d. Non-disclosure agreement

19. _____ and benefits in kind are various non-wage compensations provided to employees in addition to their normal wages or salaries. Where an employee exchanges (cash) wages for some other form of benefit, this is generally referred to as a 'salary sacrifice' arrangement. In most countries, most kinds of _____ are taxable to at least some degree.
    a. Employee benefits
    b. A Stake in the Outcome
    c. Interactive Accommodation Process
    d. A4e

20. The U.S. _____ is a federal agency whose goal is ending employment discrimination. The _____ investigates discrimination complaints based on an individual's race, color, national origin, religion, sex, age, disability and retaliation for reporting and/or opposing a discriminatory practice. The Commission is also tasked with filing suits on behalf of alleged victim(s) of discrimination against employers and as an adjudicatory for claims of discrimination brought against federal agencies.
    a. Airbus Industrie
    b. Airbus SAS
    c. ARCO
    d. Equal Employment Opportunity Commission

21. A _____ is the lowest hourly, daily or monthly wage that employers may legally pay to employees or workers. Equivalently, it is the lowest wage at which workers may sell their labor. Although _____ laws are in effect in a great many jurisdictions, there are differences of opinion about the benefits and drawbacks of a _____.
    a. Rehn-Meidner Model
    b. Value added
    c. Deregulation
    d. Minimum wage

22. A _____ is a compensation, usually financial, received by a worker in exchange for their labor.

Compensation in terms of _____s is given to worker and compensation in terms of salary is given to employees. Compensation is a monetary benefits given to employees in returns of the services provided by them.

a. State Compensation Insurance Fund
b. Profit-sharing agreement
c. Performance-related pay
d. Wage

23. _____ is the temporary suspension or permanent termination of employment of an employee or (more commonly) a group of employees for business reasons, such as the decision that certain positions are no longer necessary or a business slow-down or interruption in work. Originally the term '_____' referred exclusively to a temporary interruption in work, as when factory work cyclically falls off. However, in recent times the term can also refer to the permanent elimination of a position.
    a. Termination of employment
    b. Retirement
    c. Layoff
    d. Wrongful dismissal

24. The _____ is the labour pool in employment. It is generally used to describe those working for a single company or industry, but can also apply to a geographic region like a city, country, state, etc. The term generally excludes the employers or management, and implies those involved in manual labour.
    a. Workforce
    b. Work-life balance
    c. Division of labour
    d. Pink-collar worker

25. _____ refers to the process of screening, and selecting qualified people for a job at an organization or firm mid- and large-size organizations and companies often retain professional recruiters or outsource some of the process to _____ agencies. External _____ is the process of attracting and selecting employees from outside the organization.

The _____ industry has four main types of agencies: employment agencies, _____ websites and job search engines, 'headhunters' for executive and professional _____, and in-house _____.

a. Referral recruitment
b. Recruitment Process Outsourcing
c. Labour hire
d. Recruitment

Chapter 13. Managing Human Resources

26. _____ is an internal recruitment method employed by organisations to identify potential candidates from their existing employees social networks. An _____ scheme encourages a company's existing employees to select and recruit the suitable candidates from their social networks. As a reward, the employer typically pays the referring employee a referral bonus.
   a. Internet recruiting
   b. Executive search
   c. Employment agency
   d. Employee referral

27. Performance Testing covers a broad range of engineering or functional evaluations where a material, product, system emphasis is on the final measurable performance characteristics.

Performance testing can refer to the assessment of the performance of a human examinee. For example, a behind-the-wheel driving test is a _____ of whether a person is able to perform the functions of a competent driver of an automobile.

   a. Performance test
   b. 28-hour day
   c. Reverse engineering
   d. 1990 Clean Air Act

28. _____ is subcontracting a process, such as product design or manufacturing, to a third-party company. The decision to outsource is often made in the interest of lowering cost or making better use of time and energy costs, redirecting or conserving energy directed at the competencies of a particular business, or to make more efficient use of land, labor, capital, (information) technology and resources. _____ became part of the business lexicon during the 1980s.
   a. Outsourcing
   b. Unemployment insurance
   c. Operant conditioning
   d. Opinion leadership

29. _____ is a term defined by the Oxford English Dictionary as an individual's 'course or progress through life '. It is usually considered to pertain to remunerative work (and sometimes also formal education.)

The etymology of the term is somewhat ironic in that it comes from the Latin word carrera, which means race .

a. Nursing shortage
b. Spatial mismatch
c. Career planning
d. Career

30. In organizational development (or OD), the study of _____ looks at:

- how individuals manage their careers within and between organizations
- and how organizations structure the career progress of their members, it can also be tied into succession planning within some organizations.

In personal development, _____ is:

- '... the total constellation of psychological, sociological, educational, physical, economic, and chance factors that combine to influence the nature and significance of work in the total lifespan of any given individual.'

- '... the lifelong psychological and behavioral processes as well as contextual influences shaping one's career over the life span. As such, _____ involves the person's creation of a career pattern, decision-making style, integration of life roles, values expression, and life-role self concepts.'

Figures in _____

- Jeff A. Brown
- Jesse B. Davis
- Caela Farren
- John L. Holland
- Kris Magnusson
- Frank Parsons
- Vance Peavy
- Edgar Schein
- Rino Schreuder
- Mark L. Savickas
- Donald Super

a. Horizontal integration
b. Sole proprietorship
c. Business process reengineering
d. Career development

Chapter 13. Managing Human Resources

31. There are two types of _____ relationships: formal and informal. Informal relationships develop on their own between partners. Formal _____, on the other hand, refers to assigned relationships, often associated with organizational _____ programs designed to promote employee development or to assist at-risk children and youth.
    a. Fix it twice
    b. Human resource management system
    c. Mentoring
    d. Real Property Administrator

32. _____ is a method by which the job performance of an employee is evaluated _____ is a part of career development.

_____s are regular reviews of employee performance within organizations

Generally, the aims of a _____ are to:

- Give feedback on performance to employees.
- Identify employee training needs.
- Document criteria used to allocate organizational rewards.
- Form a basis for personnel decisions: salary increases, promotions, disciplinary actions, etc.
- Provide the opportunity for organizational diagnosis and development.
- Facilitate communication between employee and administraton
- Validate selection techniques and human resource policies to meet federal Equal Employment Opportunity requirements.

A common approach to assessing performance is to use a numerical or scalar rating system whereby managers are asked to score an individual against a number of objectives/attributes. In some companies, employees receive assessments from their manager, peers, subordinates and customers while also performing a self assessment.

   a. Progressive discipline
   b. Performance appraisal
   c. Human resource management
   d. Personnel management

33. In the fields of science, engineering, industry and statistics, _____ is the degree of closeness of a measured or calculated quantity to its actual (true) value. _____ is closely related to precision, also called reproducibility or repeatability, the degree to which further measurements or calculations show the same or similar results. _____ indicates proximity to the true value, precision to the repeatability or reproducibility of the measurement

The results of calculations or a measurement can be accurate but not precise, precise but not accurate, neither, or both.

Chapter 13. Managing Human Resources

a. AAAI
b. A4e
c. Accuracy
d. A Stake in the Outcome

34. The _____ system was developed by AMD in the mid-1990s as a method of comparing their x86 processors to those of rival Intel.

The first use of the _____ system was in 1996, when AMD used it to assert that their AMD 5x86 processor was as fast as a Pentium running at 75 MHz. The designation 'P75' was added to the chip to denote this.

a. 33 Strategies of War
b. Performance rating
c. 1990 Clean Air Act
d. 28-hour day

35. _____ describes the situation when output from (or information about the result of) an event or phenomenon in the past will influence the same event/phenomenon in the present or future. When an event is part of a chain of cause-and-effect that forms a circuit or loop, then the event is said to 'feed back' into itself.

_____ is also a synonym for:

- _____ signal; the information about the initial event that is the basis for subsequent modification of the event.
- _____ loop; the causal path that leads from the initial generation of the _____ signal to the subsequent modification of the event.

_____ is a mechanism, process or signal that is looped back to control a system within itself. Such a loop is called a _____ loop.

a. Positive feedback
b. Feedback loop
c. Feedback
d. 1990 Clean Air Act

36. A _____ is a set of categories designed to elicit information about a quantitative or a qualitative attribute. In the social sciences, common examples are the Likert scale and 1-10 _____ s in which a person selects the number which is considered to reflect the perceived quality of a product.

A _____ is an instrument that requires the rater to assign the rated object that have numerals assigned to them.

a. Thurstone scale
b. Spearman-Brown prediction formula
c. Polytomous Rasch model
d. Rating scale

37. In a human resources context, _____ or labor _____ is the rate at which an employer gains and loses employees. Simple ways to describe it are 'how long employees tend to stay' or 'the rate of traffic through the revolving door.' _____ is measured for individual companies and for their industry as a whole. If an employer is said to have a high _____ relative to its competitors, it means that employees of that company have a shorter average tenure than those of other companies in the same industry.

a. Ten year occupational employment projection
b. Continuous
c. Career portfolios
d. Turnover

38. In economics and sociology, an _____ is any factor (financial or non-financial) that enables or motivates a particular course of action, or counts as a reason for preferring one choice to the alternatives. It is an expectation that encourages people to behave in a certain way. Since human beings are purposeful creatures, the study of _____ structures is central to the study of all economic activity (both in terms of individual decision-making and in terms of co-operation and competition within a larger institutional structure.)

a. Incentive
b. AAAI
c. A4e
d. A Stake in the Outcome

39. A _____ is a research instrument consisting of a series of questions and other prompts for the purpose of gathering information from respondents. Although they are often designed for statistical analysis of the responses, this is not always the case. The _____ was invented by Sir Francis Galton.

a. Structured interview
b. Mystery shoppers
c. Questionnaire construction
d. Questionnaire

Chapter 14. Motivating Employees

1. In organizational development (OD), _____ is the application of Socio-Technical Systems principles and techniques to the humanization of work.

   The aims of _____ to improved job satisfaction, to improved through-put, to improved quality and to reduced employee problems, e.g., grievances, absenteeism.

   Under scientific management people would be directed by reason and the problems of industrial unrest would be appropriately (i.e., scientifically) addressed.

   a. Work design
   b. Path-goal theory
   c. Graduate recruitment
   d. Management process

2. A _____ is the term given to a company that facilitates the learning of its members and continuously transforms itself. _____s develop as a result of the pressures facing modern organizations and enables them to remain competitive in the business environment. A _____ has five main features; systems thinking, personal mastery, mental models, shared vision and team learning.
   a. 1990 Clean Air Act
   b. Hoshin Kanri
   c. Quality function deployment
   d. Learning organization

3. _____ has become one of the most popular theories in organizational psychology.

   Goal setting has been a formula used for acheivement since the early 1800s. The form and pattern has cahanged drastically over the years and there is still much debate as to what is the most efective pattern to follow.

   a. Human relations
   b. Corporate Culture
   c. Job satisfaction
   d. Goal-setting theory

4. _____ is a process of agreeing upon objectives within an organization so that management and employees agree to the objectives and understand what they are in the organization.

   The term '_____' was first popularized by Peter Drucker in his 1954 book 'The Practice of Management'.

   The essence of _____ is participative goal setting, choosing course of actions and decision making.

Chapter 14. Motivating Employees

109

a. Job enrichment
b. Management by objectives
c. Business economics
d. Clean sheet review

5. In economics and sociology, an _____ is any factor (financial or non-financial) that enables or motivates a particular course of action, or counts as a reason for preferring one choice to the alternatives. It is an expectation that encourages people to behave in a certain way. Since human beings are purposeful creatures, the study of _____ structures is central to the study of all economic activity (both in terms of individual decision-making and in terms of co-operation and competition within a larger institutional structure.)

a. AAAI
b. A Stake in the Outcome
c. A4e
d. Incentive

6. _____ describes the situation when output from (or information about the result of) an event or phenomenon in the past will influence the same event/phenomenon in the present or future. When an event is part of a chain of cause-and-effect that forms a circuit or loop, then the event is said to 'feed back' into itself.

_____ is also a synonym for:

- _____ signal; the information about the initial event that is the basis for subsequent modification of the event.
- _____ loop; the causal path that leads from the initial generation of the _____ signal to the subsequent modification of the event.

_____ is a mechanism, process or signal that is looped back to control a system within itself. Such a loop is called a _____ loop.

a. Feedback loop
b. Positive feedback
c. 1990 Clean Air Act
d. Feedback

7. _____ involves establishing specific, measurable and time-targeted objectives. Work on the theory of goal-setting suggests that it's an effective tool for making progress by ensuring that participants in a group with a common goal are clearly aware of what is expected from them if an objective is to be achieved. On a personal level, setting goals is a process that allows people to specify then work towards their own objectives - most commonly with financial or career-based goals.

a. Catfish effect
b. Resource-based view
c. Digital strategy
d. Goal setting

8. _____ is the use of empirically demonstrated behavior change techniques to improve behavior, such as altering an individual's behaviors and reactions to stimuli through positive and negative reinforcement of adaptive behavior and/or the reduction of maladaptive behavior through punishment and/or therapy.

The first use of the term _____ appears to have been by Edward Thorndike in 1911

a. 33 Strategies of War
b. 1990 Clean Air Act
c. 28-hour day
d. Behavior modification

9. In operant conditioning, _____ occurs when an event following a response causes an increase in the probability of that response occurring in the future. Response strength can be assessed by measures such as the frequency with which the response is made (for example, a pigeon may peck a key more times in the session), or the speed with which it is made (for example, a rat may run a maze faster.) The environment change contingent upon the response is called a reinforcer.
a. Meetings, Incentives, Conferences, and Exhibitions
b. Reinforcement
c. Diminishing Manufacturing Sources and Material Shortages
d. Historiometry

10. _____ is about the mental processes regarding choice, or choosing. It explains the processes that an individual undergoes to make choices. In organizational behavior study, _____ is a motivation theory first proposed by Victor Vroom of the Yale School of Management.
a. A4e
b. AAAI
c. A Stake in the Outcome
d. Expectancy theory

11. A _____ is a research instrument consisting of a series of questions and other prompts for the purpose of gathering information from respondents. Although they are often designed for statistical analysis of the responses, this is not always the case. The _____ was invented by Sir Francis Galton.

a. Questionnaire
b. Mystery shoppers
c. Questionnaire construction
d. Structured interview

12. In business and accounting, _____s are everything of value that is owned by a person or company. Any property or object of value that one possesses, usually considered as applicable to the payment of one's debts is considered an _____. Simplistically stated, _____s are things of value that can be readily converted into cash.
   a. Asset
   b. AAAI
   c. A Stake in the Outcome
   d. A4e

13. _____ are job factors that can cause dissatisfaction if missing but do not necessarily motivate employees if increased.

_____ have mostly to do with the job environment. These factors are important or notable only when they are lacking.

   a. Split shift
   b. Work system
   c. Work-at-home scheme
   d. Hygiene factors

14. _____ was developed by Frederick Herzberg, a psychologist who found that job satisfaction and job dissatisfaction acted independently of each other. _____ states that there are certain factors in the workplace that cause job satisfaction, while a separate set of factors cause dissatisfaction.
   a. Need for power
   b. Two-factor theory
   c. Need for Achievement
   d. 1990 Clean Air Act

15. In a human resources context, _____ or labor _____ is the rate at which an employer gains and loses employees. Simple ways to describe it are 'how long employees tend to stay' or 'the rate of traffic through the revolving door.' _____ is measured for individual companies and for their industry as a whole. If an employer is said to have a high _____ relative to its competitors, it means that employees of that company have a shorter average tenure than those of other companies in the same industry.

a. Turnover
b. Career portfolios
c. Ten year occupational employment projection
d. Continuous

16. _____ attempts to explain relational satisfaction in terms of perceptions of fair/unfair distributions of resources within interpersonal relationships. _____ is considered as one of the justice theories, It was first developed in 1962 by John Stacey Adams, a workplace and behavioral psychologist, who asserted that employees seek to maintain equity between the inputs that they bring to a job and the outcomes that they receive from it against the perceived inputs and outcomes of others (Adams, 1965.) The belief is that people value fair treatment which causes them to be motivated to keep the fairness maintained within the relationships of their co-workers and the organization.
   a. A Stake in the Outcome
   b. A4e
   c. AAAI
   d. Equity theory

17. The _____ captures an expanded spectrum of values and criteria for measuring organizational success: economic, ecological and social. With the ratification of the United Nations and ICLEI _____ standard for urban and community accounting in early 2007, this became the dominant approach to public sector full cost accounting. Similar UN standards apply to natural capital and human capital measurement to assist in measurements required by _____, e.g. the ecoBudget standard for reporting ecological footprint.
   a. 1990 Clean Air Act
   b. 33 Strategies of War
   c. 28-hour day
   d. Triple bottom line

18. The _____ 1970 is an Act of the United Kingdom Parliament which prohibits any less favourable treatment between men and women in terms of pay and conditions of employment. It came into force on 29 December 1975. The term pay is interpreted in a broad sense to include, on top of wages, things like holidays, pension rights, company perks and some kinds of bonuses.
   a. Oncale v. Sundowner Offshore Services
   b. Australian labour law
   c. Architectural Barriers Act of 1968
   d. Equal Pay Act

19. _____ is how top executives of business corporations are paid. This includes a basic salary, bonuses, shares, options and other company benefits. Over the past three decades, _____ has risen dramatically beyond the rising levels of an average worker's wage.

a. Executive compensation
b. Anti-leadership
c. Evidence-based management
d. Association management company

20. Maslow's _____ is a theory in psychology, proposed by Abraham Maslow in his 1943 paper A Theory of Human Motivation, which he subsequently extended to include his observations of humans' innate curiosity.

Maslow's _____ is predetermined in order of importance. It is often depicted as a pyramid consisting of five levels: the lowest level is associated with physiological needs, while the uppermost level is associated with self-actualization needs, particularly those related to identity and purpose. Deficiency needs must be met first. Once these are met, seeking to satisfy growth needs drives personal growth. The higher needs in this hierarchy only come into focus when the lower needs in the pyramid are met.

a. 28-hour day
b. 1990 Clean Air Act
c. Hierarchy of needs
d. 33 Strategies of War

21. In law, _____ is the term to describe a partnership between two or more parties.

In England a number of statutes on the subject have been passed, the chief being the Bastardy Act of 1845, and the Bastardy Laws Amendment Acts of 1872 and 1873. The mother of a bastard may summon the putative father to petty sessions within twelve months of the birth (or at any later time if he is proved to have contributed to the child's support within twelve months after the birth), and the justices, as after hearing evidence on both sides, may, if the mother's evidence be corroborated in some material particular, adjudge the man to be the putative father of the child, and order him to pay a sum not exceeding five shillings a week for its maintenance, together with a sum for expenses incidental to the birth, or the funeral expenses, if it has died before the date of order, and the costs of the proceedings.

a. Affiliation
b. Abraham Harold Maslow
c. Affirmative action
d. Adam Smith

22. _____ is a term that has been used in various psychology theories, often in slightly different ways (e.g., Goldstein, Maslow, Rogers.) The term was originally introduced by the organismic theorist Kurt Goldstein for the motive to realise all of one's potentialities. In his view, it is the master motive--indeed, the only real motive a person has, all others being merely manifestations of it.

a. Self-actualization
b. 33 Strategies of War
c. 28-hour day
d. 1990 Clean Air Act

Chapter 15. Dynamics of Leadership

1. _____ has been described as the 'process of social influence in which one person can enlist the aid and support of others in the accomplishment of a common task' . A definition more inclusive of followers comes from Alan Keith of Genentech who said '_____ is ultimately about creating a way for people to contribute to making something extraordinary happen.'

_____ is one of the most salient aspects of the organizational context. However, defining _____ has been challenging.

   a. Situational leadership
   b. 28-hour day
   c. 1990 Clean Air Act
   d. Leadership

2. _____ , often measured as an _____ Quotient (EQ), is a term that describes the ability, capacity, skill or (in the case of the trait _____ model) a self-perceived ability, to identify, assess, and manage the emotions of one's self, of others, and of groups. Different models have been proposed for the definition of _____ and disagreement exists as to how the term should be used. Despite these disagreements, which are often highly technical, the ability _____ and trait _____ models (but not the mixed models) are enjoying considerable support in the literature and have successful applications in many different domains.
   a. A Stake in the Outcome
   b. Emotional intelligence
   c. AAAI
   d. A4e

3. Social consciousness is consciousness shared within a society. It can also be defined as _____; to be aware of the problems that different societies and communities face on a day-to-day basis; to be conscious of the difficulties and hardships of society.

There is debate as to exactly what the term means.

   a. Soft skill
   b. Social awareness
   c. Self-disclosure
   d. Role conflict

4. In behaviorial science, system theory and dynamic systems modeling, a _____ reproduces the required behavior of the original analyzed system, such as there is a one-to-one correspondence between the behavior of the original system and the simulated system. That namely implies that the model uniquely predicts future system states from past systems states. The behavioral approach is motivated by the aim of obtaining a framework for system analysis that respects the underlying physics and sets up the appropriate mathematical concepts from there.

a. 1990 Clean Air Act
b. 28-hour day
c. 33 Strategies of War
d. Behavioral model

5. _____ and Theory Y are theories of human motivation created and developed by Douglas McGregor at the MIT Sloan School of Management in the 1960s that have been used in human resource management, organizational behavior, organizational communication and organizational development. They describe two very different attitudes toward workforce motivation. McGregor felt that companies followed either one or the other approach.

In _____, which many managers practice, management assumes employees are inherently lazy and will avoid work if they can. They inherently dislike work. Because of this, workers need to be closely supervised and comprehensive systems of controls developed.

a. Theory X
b. Cash cow
c. Management team
d. Job enrichment

6. Theory X and _____ are theories of human motivation created and developed by Douglas McGregor at the MIT Sloan School of Management in the 1960s that have been used in human resource management, organizational behavior, organizational communication and organizational development. They describe two very different attitudes toward workforce motivation. McGregor felt that companies followed either one or the other approach.

In _____, management assumes employees may be ambitious and self-motivated and exercise self-control. It is believed that employees enjoy their mental and physical work duties.

a. Contingency theory
b. Theory Y
c. Business Workflow Analysis
d. Design leadership

7. _____ of the learning curve effect and the closely related experience curve effect express the relationship between equations for experience and efficiency or between efficiency gains and investment in the effort. The experience of 'learning curves' was first observed by the 19th Century German psychologist Hermann Ebbinghaus according to the difficulty of memorizing varying numbers of verbal stimuli, and subsequent learning about the complex processes of learning are discussed in the

Chapter 15. Dynamics of Leadership

The rule used for representing the learning curve effect states that the more times a task has been performed, the less time will be required on each subsequent iteration.

a. Distribution
b. Spatial Decision Support Systems
c. Point biserial correlation coefficient
d. Models

8. A _____ is a name or trademark connected with a product or producer. _____s have become increasingly important components of culture and the economy, now being described as 'cultural accessories and personal philosophies'.

Some people distinguish the psychological aspect of a _____ from the experiential aspect.

a. Brand awareness
b. Brand loyalty
c. Brand extension
d. Brand

9. Some people distinguish the psychological aspect of a brand from the experiential aspect. The experiential aspect consists of the sum of all points of contact with the brand and is known as the brand experience. The psychological aspect, sometimes referred to as the _____, is a symbolic construct created within the minds of people and consists of all the information and expectations associated with a product or service.

a. Channel conflict
b. Brand management
c. Brand awareness
d. Brand image

10. An _____ is software that attempts to reproduce the performance of one or more human experts, most commonly in a specific problem domain, and is a traditional application and/or subfield of artificial intelligence. A wide variety of methods can be used to simulate the performance of the expert however common to most or all are 1) the creation of a so-called 'knowledgebase' which uses some knowledge representation formalism to capture the Subject Matter Experts (SME) knowledge and 2) a process of gathering that knowledge from the SME and codifying it according to the formalism, which is called knowledge engineering. _____s may or may not have learning components but a third common element is that once the system is developed it is proven by being placed in the same real world problem solving situation as the human SME, typically as an aid to human workers or a supplement to some information system.

a. A Stake in the Outcome
b. Expert System
c. AAAI
d. A4e

11. In economics, business, retail, and accounting, a _____ is the value of money that has been used up to produce something, and hence is not available for use anymore. In economics, a _____ is an alternative that is given up as a result of a decision. In business, the _____ may be one of acquisition, in which case the amount of money expended to acquire it is counted as _____.
   a. Cost overrun
   b. Cost allocation
   c. Fixed costs
   d. Cost

12. _____ is a leadership style that defines as leadership that creates voluble and positive change in the followers. A transformational leader focuses on 'transforming' others to help each other, to look out for each other, be encouraging, harmonious, and look out for the organization as a whole. In this leadership, the leader enhances the motivation, moral and performance of his follower group.
   a. Strong-Campbell Interest Inventory
   b. SESAMO
   c. Transformational Leadership
   d. Polynomial conjoint measurement

13. There are two types of _____ relationships: formal and informal. Informal relationships develop on their own between partners. Formal _____, on the other hand, refers to assigned relationships, often associated with organizational _____ programs designed to promote employee development or to assist at-risk children and youth.
   a. Human resource management system
   b. Real Property Administrator
   c. Mentoring
   d. Fix it twice

14. _____ in its literal sense is the process of transformation of local or regional phenomena into global ones. It can be described as a process by which the people of the world are unified into a single society and function together.

This process is a combination of economic, technological, sociocultural and political forces.

Chapter 15. Dynamics of Leadership

   a. Cost Management
   b. Histogram
   c. Collaborative Planning, Forecasting and Replenishment
   d. Globalization

15. _____ was developed by Frederick Herzberg, a psychologist who found that job satisfaction and job dissatisfaction acted independently of each other. _____ states that there are certain factors in the workplace that cause job satisfaction, while a separate set of factors cause dissatisfaction.
   a. Need for power
   b. Two-factor theory
   c. 1990 Clean Air Act
   d. Need for Achievement

16. A _____ is a research instrument consisting of a series of questions and other prompts for the purpose of gathering information from respondents. Although they are often designed for statistical analysis of the responses, this is not always the case. The _____ was invented by Sir Francis Galton.
   a. Questionnaire
   b. Questionnaire construction
   c. Structured interview
   d. Mystery shoppers

Chapter 16. Communicating Effectively

1. The term _____ was introduced by anthropologist Edward T. Hall in 1966 to describe set measurable distances between people as they interact. The effects of _____, according to Hall, can be summarized by the following loose rule:

According to Jonathon Tabor distance-spacing theories based on the early animal-like human of German zoologist Heini Hediger, as found in his 1955 book Studies of the Behavior of Captive Animals in Zoos and Circuses. Hediger, in animals, had distinguished between flight distance , critical distance (attack boundary), personal distance (distance separating members of non-contact species, as a pair of swans), and social distance (intraspecies communication distance.)

   a. Proxemics
   b. 33 Strategies of War
   c. 1990 Clean Air Act
   d. 28-hour day

2. _____ are legal property rights over creations of the mind, both artistic and commercial, and the corresponding fields of law. Under _____ law, owners are granted certain exclusive rights to a variety of intangible assets, such as musical, literary, and artistic works; ideas, discoveries and inventions; and words, phrases, symbols, and designs. Common types of _____ include copyrights, trademarks, patents, industrial design rights and trade secrets.
   a. Intent
   b. Equal Pay Act
   c. Intellectual property
   d. Unemployment Action Center

3. _____ plant, and equipment, is a term used in accountancy for assets and property which cannot easily be converted into cash. This can be compared with current assets such as cash or bank accounts, which are described as liquid assets. In most cases, only tangible assets are referred to as fixed.
   a. 33 Strategies of War
   b. 1990 Clean Air Act
   c. 28-hour day
   d. Fixed asset

4. A _____ is a form of qualitative research in which a group of people are asked about their attitude towards a product, service, concept, advertisement, idea, or packaging. Questions are asked in an interactive group setting where participants are free to talk with other group members.

The first _____s were created at the Bureau of Applied Social Research by associate director, sociologist Robert K. Merton.

a. 1990 Clean Air Act
b. Market analysis
c. Marketing research
d. Focus group

5. _____ describes the situation when output from (or information about the result of) an event or phenomenon in the past will influence the same event/phenomenon in the present or future. When an event is part of a chain of cause-and-effect that forms a circuit or loop, then the event is said to 'feed back' into itself.

_____ is also a synonym for:

- _____ signal; the information about the initial event that is the basis for subsequent modification of the event.
- _____ loop; the causal path that leads from the initial generation of the _____ signal to the subsequent modification of the event.

_____ is a mechanism, process or signal that is looped back to control a system within itself. Such a loop is called a _____ loop.

a. Feedback
b. Feedback loop
c. 1990 Clean Air Act
d. Positive feedback

6. A _____ is a research instrument consisting of a series of questions and other prompts for the purpose of gathering information from respondents. Although they are often designed for statistical analysis of the responses, this is not always the case. The _____ was invented by Sir Francis Galton.
a. Mystery shoppers
b. Structured interview
c. Questionnaire construction
d. Questionnaire

Chapter 17. Working in Teams

1. In commerce, _____ is the length of time it takes from a product being conceived until its being available for sale. _____ is important in industries where products are outmoded quickly. A common assumption is that _____ matters most for first-of-a-kind products, but actually the leader often has the luxury of time, while the clock is clearly running for the followers.

    a. Time to market
    b. Market entry
    c. Procurement
    d. Career development

2. A _____ is a volunteer group composed of workers (or even students), usually under the leadership of their supervisor (but they can elect a team leader), who are trained to identify, analyse and solve work-related problems and present their solutions to management in order to improve the performance of the organization, and motivate and enrich the work of employees. When matured, true _____s become self-managing, having gained the confidence of management.
    _____s are an alternative to the dehumanising concept of the Division of Labour, where workers or individuals are treated like robots.

    a. Quality circle
    b. Certified in Production and Inventory Management
    c. Connectionist expert systems
    d. Competency-based job descriptions

3. _____ is a business management strategy aimed at embedding awareness of quality in all organizational processes. _____ has been widely used in manufacturing, education, hospitals, call centers, government, and service industries, as well as NASA space and science programs.

    As defined by the International Organization for Standardization (ISO):

    '_____ is a management approach for an organization, centered on quality, based on the participation of all its members and aiming at long-term success through customer satisfaction, and benefits to all members of the organization and to society.' ISO 8402:1994

    One major aim is to reduce variation from every process so that greater consistency of effort is obtained. (Royse, D., Thyer, B., Padgett D., ' Logan T., 2006)

    a. 1990 Clean Air Act
    b. Total quality management
    c. Quality management
    d. 28-hour day

Chapter 17. Working in Teams

4. In business and engineering, new _____ is the term used to describe the complete process of bringing a new product or service to market. There are two parallel paths involved in the NProduct development process: one involves the idea generation, product design, and detail engineering; the other involves market research and marketing analysis. Companies typically see new _____ as the first stage in generating and commercializing new products within the overall strategic process of product life cycle management used to maintain or grow their market share.

a. 1990 Clean Air Act
b. 33 Strategies of War
c. 28-hour day
d. Product development

5. _____ is a civil designation for persons who are incorporated in a fixed or permanent way to a society or group: regular member of the working staff, permanent staff distinguished from a supernumerary.

The term '_____' and its counterpart, 'supernumerary,' originated in Spanish and Latin American academy and government; it is now also used in countries all over the world, such as France, the U.S., England, Italy, etc.

There are _____ members of surgical organizations, of universities, of gastronomical associations, etc.

a. Adam Smith
b. Abraham Harold Maslow
c. Affiliation
d. Numerary

6. _____ is a type of thought exhibited by group members who try to minimize conflict and reach consensus without critically testing, analyzing, and evaluating ideas. Individual creativity, uniqueness, and independent thinking are lost in the pursuit of group cohesiveness, as are the advantages of reasonable balance in choice and thought that might normally be obtained by making decisions as a group. During _____, members of the group avoid promoting viewpoints outside the comfort zone of consensus thinking.

a. Diffusion of responsibility
b. Psychological statistics
c. Self-report inventory
d. Groupthink

7. _____ has been described as the 'process of social influence in which one person can enlist the aid and support of others in the accomplishment of a common task'. A definition more inclusive of followers comes from Alan Keith of Genentech who said '_____ is ultimately about creating a way for people to contribute to making something extraordinary happen.'

_____ is one of the most salient aspects of the organizational context. However, defining _____ has been challenging.

Chapter 17. Working in Teams

a. 1990 Clean Air Act
b. 28-hour day
c. Situational leadership
d. Leadership

8. _____ can be regarded as an outcome of mental processes (cognitive process) leading to the selection of a course of action among several alternatives. Every _____ process produces a final choice. The output can be an action or an opinion of choice.

a. 1990 Clean Air Act
b. Decision making
c. 33 Strategies of War
d. 28-hour day

9. _____ are a class of electronic meeting systems, a collaboration technology designed to support meetings and group work. _____ are distinct from computer supported cooperative work (CSCW) technologies as _____ are more focused on task support, whereas CSCW tools provide general communication support.

_____ were referred to as a Group Support System (GSS) or an electronic meeting system since they shared similar foundations.

a. Learning organization
b. Hoshin Kanri
c. 1990 Clean Air Act
d. Group decision support systems

10. _____ constitute a class of computer-based information systems including knowledge-based systems that support decision-making activities.

_____ are a specific class of computerized information systems that supports business and organizational decision-making activities. A properly-designed _____ is an interactive software-based system intended to help decision makers compile useful information from raw data, documents, personal knowledge, and/or business models to identify and solve problems and make decisions.

a. 28-hour day
b. 1990 Clean Air Act
c. Spatial Decision Support Systems
d. Decision support systems

Chapter 17. Working in Teams

11. In neuroscience, the _____ is a collection of brain structures which attempts to regulate and control behavior by inducing pleasurable effects.

A psychological reward is a process that reinforces behavior -- something that, when offered, causes a behavior to increase in intensity. Reward is an operational concept for describing the positive value an individual ascribes to an object, behavioral act or an internal physical state.

a. 1990 Clean Air Act
b. 28-hour day
c. 33 Strategies of War
d. Reward system

12. A _____ -- also known as a geographically dispersed team -- is a group of individuals who work across time, space, and organizational boundaries with links strengthened by webs of communication technology. They have complementary skills and are committed to a common purpose, have interdependent performance goals, and share an approach to work for which they hold themselves mutually accountable. Geographically dispersed teams allow organizations to hire and retain the best people regardless of location.

a. Trademark
b. Kanban
c. Risk management
d. Virtual Team

13. The _____ is a performance management tool for measuring whether the smaller-scale operational activities of a company are aligned with its larger-scale objectives in terms of vision and strategy.

By focusing not only on financial outcomes but also on the operational, marketing and developmental inputs to these, the _____ helps provide a more comprehensive view of a business, which in turn helps organizations act in their best long-term interests. This tool is also being used to address business response to climate change and greenhouse gas emissions.

a. Middle management
b. Balanced scorecard
c. Management development
d. Commercial management

Chapter 18. Understanding Organizational Culture and Cultural Diversity

1. The 'business case for _____', theorizes that in a global marketplace, a company that employs a diverse workforce (both men and women, people of many generations, people from ethnically and racially diverse backgrounds etc.) is better able to understand the demographics of the marketplace it serves and is thus better equipped to thrive in that marketplace than a company that has a more limited range of employee demographics.

An additional corollary suggests that a company that supports the _____ of its workforce can also improve employee satisfaction, productivity and retention.

   a. Trademark
   b. Diversity
   c. Kanban
   d. Virtual team

2. _____ is an idea in the field of Organizational studies and management which describes the psychology, attitudes, experiences, beliefs and Values (personal and cultural values) of an organization. It has been defined as 'the specific collection of values and norms that are shared by people and groups in an organization and that control the way they interact with each other and with stakeholders outside the organization.'

This definition continues to explain organizational values also known as 'beliefs and ideas about what kinds of goals members of an organization should pursue and ideas about the appropriate kinds or standards of behavior organizational members should use to achieve these goals. From organizational values develop organizational norms, guidelines or expectations that prescribe appropriate kinds of behavior by employees in particular situations and control the behavior of organizational members towards one another.'

_____ is not the same as corporate culture.

   a. Organizational culture
   b. Union shop
   c. Organizational effectiveness
   d. Organizational development

3. In sociology, anthropology and cultural studies, a _____ is a group of people with a culture (whether distinct or hidden) which differentiates them from the larger culture to which they belong. If a particular _____ is characterized by a systematic opposition to the dominant culture, it may be described as a counterculture.

As early as 1950, David Riesman distinguished between a majority, 'which passively accepted commercially provided styles and meanings, and a '_____' which actively sought a minority style ...

a. 1990 Clean Air Act
b. Subculture
c. 33 Strategies of War
d. 28-hour day

4. Organizational culture is not the same as _____. It is wider and deeper concepts, something that an organization 'is' rather than what it 'has' (according to Buchanan and Huczynski.)

_____ is the total sum of the values, customs, traditions and meanings that make a company unique.

a. Job analysis
b. Path-goal theory
c. Corporate culture
d. Work design

5. A _____ or labor union is an organization of workers who have banded together to achieve common goals in key areas and working conditions. The _____, through its leadership, bargains with the employer on behalf of union members (rank and file members) and negotiates labor contracts (Collective bargaining) with employers. This may include the negotiation of wages, work rules, complaint procedures, rules governing hiring, firing and promotion of workers, benefits, workplace safety and policies.
a. Company union
b. Trade union
c. Working time
d. Labour law

6. The phrase mergers and _____ s refers to the aspect of corporate strategy, corporate finance and management dealing with the buying, selling and combining of different companies that can aid, finance, or help a growing company in a given industry grow rapidly without having to create another business entity.

An _____, also known as a takeover or a buyout, is the buying of one company (the 'target') by another. An _____ may be friendly or hostile.

a. AAAI
b. Acquisition
c. A Stake in the Outcome
d. A4e

Chapter 18. Understanding Organizational Culture and Cultural Diversity

7. The phrase _____ refers to the aspect of corporate strategy, corporate finance and management dealing with the buying, selling and combining of different companies that can aid, finance, or help a growing company in a given industry grow rapidly without having to create another business entity.

An acquisition, also known as a takeover or a buyout, is the buying of one company (the 'target') by another. An acquisition may be friendly or hostile.

   a. 33 Strategies of War
   b. Mergers and acquisitions
   c. 1990 Clean Air Act
   d. 28-hour day

8. _____ or _____ data refers to selected population characteristics as used in government, marketing or opinion research, or the _____ profiles used in such research. Note the distinction from the term 'demography' Commonly-used _____s include race, age, income, disabilities, mobility (in terms of travel time to work or number of vehicles available), educational attainment, home ownership, employment status, and even location.
   a. Affiliation
   b. Adam Smith
   c. Demographic
   d. Abraham Harold Maslow

9. The _____ is the labour pool in employment. It is generally used to describe those working for a single company or industry, but can also apply to a geographic region like a city, country, state, etc. The term generally excludes the employers or management, and implies those involved in manual labour.
   a. Work-life balance
   b. Division of labour
   c. Pink-collar worker
   d. Workforce

10.

The terms _____ and positive action refer to policies that take race, ethnicity, or gender into consideration in an attempt to promote equal opportunity. The focus of such policies ranges from employment and education to public contracting and health programs. The impetus towards _____ is twofold: to maximize diversity in all levels of society, along with its presumed benefits, and to redress perceived disadvantages due to overt, institutional, or involuntary discrimination.

a. Affirmative action
b. Abraham Harold Maslow
c. Affiliation
d. Adam Smith

11. _____ is a contract between two parties, one being the employer and the other being the employee. An employee may be defined as: 'A person in the service of another under any contract of hire, express or implied, oral or written, where the employer has the power or right to control and direct the employee in the material details of how the work is to be performed.' Black's Law Dictionary page 471 (5th ed. 1979.)
   a. Exit interview
   b. Employment rate
   c. Employment counsellor
   d. Employment

12. _____ is the body of laws, administrative rulings, and precedents which address the legal rights of, and restrictions on, working people and their organizations. As such, it mediates many aspects of the relationship between trade unions, employers and employees. In Canada, employment laws related to unionized workplaces are differentiated from those relating to particular individuals.
   a. Four-day week
   b. Shift work
   c. Trade union
   d. Labor law

13. The general definition of an _____ is an evaluation of a person, organization, system, process, project or product. _____s are performed to ascertain the validity and reliability of information; also to provide an assessment of a system's internal control. The goal of an _____ is to express an opinion on the person / organization/system (etc) in question, under evaluation based on work done on a test basis.
   a. Audit
   b. Audit committee
   c. A Stake in the Outcome
   d. Internal control

14. A _____ is a form of qualitative research in which a group of people are asked about their attitude towards a product, service, concept, advertisement, idea, or packaging. Questions are asked in an interactive group setting where participants are free to talk with other group members.

The first _____s were created at the Bureau of Applied Social Research by associate director, sociologist Robert K. Merton.

Chapter 18. Understanding Organizational Culture and Cultural Diversity

a. Marketing research
b. 1990 Clean Air Act
c. Focus group
d. Market analysis

15. The _____ is a performance management tool for measuring whether the smaller-scale operational activities of a company are aligned with its larger-scale objectives in terms of vision and strategy.

By focusing not only on financial outcomes but also on the operational, marketing and developmental inputs to these, the _____ helps provide a more comprehensive view of a business, which in turn helps organizations act in their best long-term interests. This tool is also being used to address business response to climate change and greenhouse gas emissions.

a. Middle management
b. Balanced scorecard
c. Commercial management
d. Management development

16. _____ is training for the purpose of increasing participants' cultural awareness, knowledge, and skills, which is based on the assumption that the training will benefit an organization by protecting against civil rights violations, increasing the inclusion of different identity groups, and promoting better teamwork.

_____ has been a controversial issue, due to moral considerations as well as questioned efficiency or even counterproductivity.

According to Michael Bird, many project managers may feel that they are treading new territory as they lead project teams made of individuals from different cultures, heterogeneous mixes, and differing demographics.

a. Self-disclosure
b. Soft skill
c. Diversity training
d. Role conflict

17. _____ is a concept in ethics with several meanings. It is often used synonymously with such concepts as responsibility, answerability, enforcement, blameworthiness, liability and other terms associated with the expectation of account-giving. As an aspect of governance, it has been central to discussions related to problems in both the public and private (corporation) worlds.

a. Usury
b. A4e
c. A Stake in the Outcome
d. Accountability

18. _____ is the set of processes, customs, policies, laws, and institutions affecting the way a corporation (or company) is directed, administered or controlled. _____ also includes the relationships among the many stakeholders involved and the goals for which the corporation is governed. The principal stakeholders are the shareholders/members, management, and the board of directors.
    a. No-FEAR Act
    b. Corporate governance
    c. Guarantee
    d. Flextime

Chapter 1
1. d   2. d   3. c   4. a   5. b   6. d   7. d   8. b   9. a   10. c
11. a   12. a   13. d   14. a   15. a   16. d

Chapter 2
1. b   2. d   3. d   4. c   5. a   6. d   7. d   8. b   9. a   10. b
11. b   12. d   13. d   14. d   15. d   16. b   17. d   18. d   19. a   20. c
21. d   22. c   23. d   24. d   25. d   26. b   27. c   28. c   29. d   30. a
31. b   32. b   33. c

Chapter 3
1. d   2. d   3. d   4. a   5. b   6. d   7. b   8. d   9. d   10. d
11. d   12. d   13. b   14. b   15. b   16. b   17. d   18. a   19. d   20. a
21. a   22. b

Chapter 4
1. c   2. c   3. a   4. c   5. d   6. d   7. b   8. d   9. d   10. c
11. c   12. d   13. d   14. c   15. c   16. d   17. b   18. b   19. d   20. d
21. b   22. a   23. d   24. b   25. d   26. d   27. d   28. c   29. d   30. a
31. a   32. d   33. a

Chapter 5
1. a   2. d   3. b   4. d   5. a   6. d   7. d   8. b   9. d   10. a
11. d   12. a   13. c   14. a   15. c   16. d   17. c   18. d   19. d   20. b
21. d   22. b   23. c   24. a   25. d   26. c   27. c   28. b

Chapter 6
1. d   2. d   3. b   4. d   5. d   6. d   7. b   8. a   9. d   10. d
11. b   12. d   13. d   14. b

Chapter 7
1. a   2. d   3. c   4. d   5. d   6. b   7. b   8. d   9. a   10. d
11. b   12. d   13. d   14. d   15. d   16. b   17. b   18. d   19. d   20. d
21. d   22. a   23. d   24. d   25. c   26. b   27. a   28. c   29. d   30. a

Chapter 8
1. d   2. d   3. d   4. d   5. c   6. d   7. d   8. d   9. a   10. c
11. d   12. a   13. d   14. d

Chapter 9
1. c   2. b   3. d   4. c   5. d   6. b   7. d   8. d   9. d   10. b
11. b   12. d   13. a   14. d   15. d   16. d   17. d   18. d   19. a   20. d
21. c   22. d   23. b   24. d   25. d

ANSWER KEY

Chapter 10
1. d   2. c   3. d   4. a   5. b   6. d   7. d   8. b   9. b   10. d
11. d   12. d   13. b   14. c   15. d   16. a   17. d   18. b   19. d   20. a
21. b   22. b   23. c   24. d   25. d   26. d   27. b   28. c   29. a   30. b
31. b   32. d   33. c   34. c   35. d   36. d   37. c   38. a   39. d   40. d
41. b   42. a   43. d   44. d

Chapter 11
1. c   2. a   3. d   4. a   5. c   6. a   7. c   8. d   9. d   10. a
11. a   12. b   13. d

Chapter 12
1. a   2. d   3. c   4. a   5. d   6. d   7. d   8. d   9. d   10. d
11. c   12. c   13. d   14. a   15. d   16. c   17. d   18. d   19. d   20. a
21. c   22. d   23. a   24. c   25. c   26. d   27. d

Chapter 13
1. c   2. a   3. c   4. d   5. d   6. a   7. b   8. c   9. d   10. b
11. d   12. d   13. d   14. d   15. b   16. b   17. d   18. b   19. a   20. d
21. d   22. d   23. c   24. a   25. d   26. d   27. a   28. a   29. d   30. d
31. c   32. b   33. c   34. b   35. c   36. d   37. d   38. a   39. d

Chapter 14
1. a   2. d   3. d   4. b   5. d   6. d   7. d   8. d   9. b   10. d
11. a   12. a   13. d   14. b   15. a   16. d   17. d   18. d   19. a   20. c
21. a   22. a

Chapter 15
1. d   2. b   3. b   4. d   5. a   6. b   7. d   8. d   9. d   10. b
11. d   12. c   13. c   14. d   15. b   16. a

Chapter 16
1. a   2. c   3. d   4. d   5. a   6. d

Chapter 17
1. a   2. a   3. b   4. d   5. d   6. d   7. d   8. b   9. d   10. d
11. d   12. d   13. b

Chapter 18
1. b   2. a   3. b   4. c   5. b   6. b   7. b   8. c   9. d   10. a
11. d   12. d   13. a   14. c   15. b   16. c   17. d   18. b

www.ingramcontent.com/pod-product-compliance
Lightning Source LLC
Chambersburg PA
CBHW082044230426
43670CB00016B/2770